In memory of our fathers   2003

D0626749

Copyright © 2003 by The Livingstone Corporation

All rights reserved. No portion of this book may be reproduced, stored in a retrieval sys-
tem, or transmitted in any form or by any means—electronic, mechanical, photocopy,
recording, scanning, or other—except for brief quotations in critical reviews or articles,
without the prior written permission of the publisher.

Published in Nashville, Tennessee, by Thomas Nelson, Inc.

Authors are represented by the literary agency of Alive Communications, Inc., 7680
Goddard Street, Suite 200, Colorado Springs, CO 80920.

Unless otherwise indicated, all Scripture quotations are taken from the *Holy Bible*, New
Living Translation, copyright © 1996. Used by permission of Tyndale House Publishers,
Inc., Wheaton, Illinois 60189. All rights reserved.

Scripture quotations marked NIV are taken from the HOLY BIBLE: NEW INTERNA-
TIONAL VERSION ®. Copyright © 1973, 1978, 1984 by International Bible Society.
Used by permission of Zondervan Publishing House. All rights reserved.

Produced with the assistance of The Livingstone Corporation (www.livingstonecorp.com).
Project staff includes Bruce Barton, Dave Veerman, Greg Asimakoupoulos, Kara Veerman
Conrad, and Paige Drygas.

Library of Congress Cataloging-in-Publication Data

Veerman, David.
    When your father dies : how a man deals with the loss of his father / Dave
Veerman and Bruce Barton.
        p. cm.
    Includes bibliographical references.
    ISBN 0-7852-6366-7 (hardcover)
    1. Grief. 2. Bereavement. 3. Fathers—Death—Psychological aspects. 4. Fathers
and sons. I. Barton, Bruce B. II. Title.
BF575.G7V44 2003
155.9'37'081—dc22   2003015246

Printed in the United States of America

03 04 05 06 07 BVG 5 4 3 2 1

WHEN YOUR FATHER DIES

How a Man Deals with the Loss of His Father

DAVE VEERMAN

and

BRUCE BARTON

THOMAS NELSON PUBLISHERS®
Nashville

A Division of Thomas Nelson, Inc.
www.ThomasNelson.com

WHEN YOUR
FATHER DIES

"Dave Veerman and Bruce Barton know the pain associated with losing a dad. Not only have they both experienced father loss, but they have listened, researched, and summarized the thoughts of many others. A significant addition to the growing genre of books on fatherhood, *When Your Father Dies* is insightful, balanced in its approach, and a helpful tool to anyone seeking to resolve the issues of father loss. I heartily recommend it."

> — KEN CANFIELD, PH.D.
> Founder and president,
> National Center for Fathering

"As I have talked for years with Dave and Bruce about the topic of this book, I have felt in my heart this is a tremendous need in the lives of men across our country. I am so honored to contribute my endorsement to Dave and Bruce's groundbreaking work on helping men come to grips with the loss of their father. If you have lost your own dad or if you have a good friend who has lost his father, this book is for you. It will help to close the loop on any past hurts, to keep alive the positive memories of a father, and to build that legacy for a lifetime."

> — DR. JOHN TRENT
> President of Encouraging
> Words and StrongFamilies.com

"My father ('Pop') has had such a wonderfully profound impact on my life that it defies description. On July 4, 1995, Pop died, and I was left with that weird mixture of sadness, joy, legacy, and loss. During those dark days I wish I had a 'map' to guide me. That's why I want to recommend to you *When Your Father Dies* as an excellent, important, and valuable resource. Every man needs to read this book!"

> — DR. CRAWFORD W. LORITTS JR.
> Speaker, author, radio host,
> and Associate Director of
> Campus Crusade for Christ USA

ENDORSEMENTS FOR

WHEN YOUR FATHER DIES

"This book is sure to bring solace to any man who has lost his father. *When Your Father Dies*, however, is not only a book about loss and grief. It is a book about learning from one of life's most significant jolts. Filled with psychological insight, biblical wisdom, and practical helps, this book is powerful."

— LES PARROTT, PH.D.
Seattle Pacific University
Author of *High Maintenance Relationships*

"When my own father died, a friend shared with me that 'the day a man's father dies is the most significant day in his son's life.' Other than the day of my salvation, I agree. Veerman and Barton have written *the* ground-breaking book on the topic of the loss of a man's father. If you have experienced the loss of your dad, you will be comforted. If you haven't, keep it nearby for one of the most significant passages of your own life or to give it to a man who has a grieving heart."

— DR. GARY ROSBERG
President,
America's Family Coaches
Radio cohost, speaker, and author of *Divorce Proof Your Marriage*

"I grew up in church with the Veerman family and knew Dave's dad many decades ago. There is no gift like the gift of a loving dad and no pain like the loss of one. It's an honor to endorse such a wise, tender healing treatment."

— JOHN ORTBERG
Author of *If You Want to Walk on Water, You've Got to Get Out of the Boat*

"When your Dad dies, it is always too soon, and the loss is traumatic, tearing deep into your heart. His absence changes everything—and it changes you. As you read *When Your Father Dies*, you'll reminisce and remember . . . you'll weep, smile, and laugh . . . you'll grieve and you'll heal."

— DR. TIM CLINTON
President, The American Association of Christian Counselors

For Sam Barton and Marv Veerman

Contents

CONTENTS

Introduction

Bruce and I go way back. In fact, we met in college and have stayed close ever since. We ministered together, studied together, stood up in each other's wedding, and watched our respective children grow and mature. We also know each other's family. During and after college I remember great meals and times of fellowship with Bruce's parents and sister.

Although Bruce and I both worked for Youth for Christ, he served at the National Headquarters in Illinois, and I relocated to Louisiana for a while—so we weren't as close geographically for seven years. At the end of that time, though, I was able to join him at the national office.

When Bruce told me that his father had been hospitalized and wasn't doing well, I was right there and could commiserate with him. And I was saddened because I knew Sam Barton. Then, when Bruce told me his father had died, I felt terrible, and I expressed my sincere condolences.

But I didn't attend the funeral. Why not? I lived as close to the funeral home and church as Bruce and his family. And, as I have said, Bruce and I were close friends and associates. I can't give a definitive answer, but I recall Bruce giving me "permission" not to . . . and I knew that he and his father had problems relating to each other . . . and I was pretty busy . . . and I sent a card and flowers—I had any number of reasons for not going.

Then, about a year later, *my* father died, and I became personally and painfully aware of the trauma of that experience. I also remember feeling so grateful for the relatives and friends who made the effort to come to the funeral. And I felt guilt and regret for having skipped the service for Bruce's dad.

Nothing will help you appreciate an experience as much as going though it yourself. Moving beyond a mere intellectual concept or idea, it becomes real. That's what happened in marriage and in having and rearing children. And it happened when I lost Dad. In *living* those events, ideals crashed into reality. Thus, since my father's death, I have been much more empathetic to other men going through that experience.

A few weeks later, Bruce and I had a good talk (in which I apologized profusely) about our feelings during and subsequent to the funeral, and we discovered much in common. Our experience was profound, but was it just us, or did all men go through what we did? Later, Bruce said we ought to write a book to help other men prepare for this eventuality or to help them through it. I agreed.

That was easier to say than do, however. It's not that we couldn't write—we've authored several books—and it's not that we couldn't gain an entry to a publishing house. But most of the publishers with whom we shared our idea were skeptical about the need. Only later did we realize what they had in common—the men to whom we spoke had fathers who were still living. In other words, they hadn't gone through the experience.

Some of our publishing friends expressed interest in the book, but they wanted to expand the topic (fathers and mothers) and to focus on the feelings of both men and women. They encouraged us to write about losing a parent. But we felt strongly that we should keep our original emphasis—a book about how *men* deal with the death of their *fathers*. We waited for a publisher who shared our same vision for the book, and we're grateful to Nelson Books for supporting and preserving that father-son emphasis.

You see, in discussing these experiences with other men who had lost their dads, we found that we stood on common ground. Whether the deaths were gradual and expected or sudden, unexpected jolts, and regardless of the health of the father-son relationship, each man was touched deeply and affected greatly by his father's death and was surprised by his emotions, or lack of them, and the life adjustments that followed. Many felt totally unprepared for the process they went through. Every conversation we had strengthened our conviction that there is something unique in the male experience that goes beyond grieving.

Yes, we could have written this book to a wider audience, discussing the effects of the death of a "parent" on both sons and daughters, but we've chosen to focus on the unique relationship between father and son. James Dobson writes, "In my opinion (and in the opinion of an increasing number of researchers), the father plays an essential role in a boy's normal development as a man. The truth is, Dad is more important than Mom [in this regard]. Mothers make boys. Fathers make men."[1] In other words, we men find our identity in our fathers—through heredity and, certainly, through environment—for better or worse. When a man's father dies, therefore, he loses a big piece of himself. No wonder the event can be traumatic!

This book is about those surprises and adjustments, not just about grief. It is written to help men and women better understand the deep relationship between father and son and to help men prepare for and adapt to their losses.

Each chapter focuses on a specific life experience, with personal stories of men from all walks of life and life experiences, and from a variety of races, nationalities, and locations. We wanted men to tell their stories. Men need to talk with each other, so we interviewed sixty of them. Our interviews covered the spectrum in terms of the age of both sons and fathers at the time of the death. And we spoke with men who had lived estranged from their fathers as well as those who had enjoyed close relationships. In addition to describing each need and adjustment, we have included personal insights and practical advice from our own experience, those we interviewed, and professional counselors.

We've identified the comments of the men we interviewed by their first name (and a last initial when more than one person we interviewed shared the same first name). Our personal experiences will be italicized, with the name of the person speaking (Bruce Barton or Dave Veerman) appearing afterward.

Each chapter will describe in detail an aspect of the experience and will give suggestions for growing through the experience and using it as a springboard into the rest of life. We have also included a set of questions at the end of each chapter to help you reflect on the main points of the chapter and to motivate you to take action, if necessary.

If you are one whose father has died, we hope that as a result of reading this book you will grow in your understanding of yourself and your relationship with your father, you will deepen your relationship with your children, you will be able to reach out to other men when they need it, you will help prepare your sons for when they must face your death, and you will see God at work though this difficult time in your life.

If you are reading this because a man you care about has lost his father, we hope that you will gain a deeper appreciation for what he is experiencing and, thus, will know how to respond to him and his feelings.

If your father still lives, we encourage and challenge you to make the most of the living years. We pray that this book will help.

—DAVE VEERMAN

1

REALITY CHECK
Acknowledging the Truth

What a great retreat it has been: colorful autumn leaves, clear skies, cool days, crisp nights—and an afternoon touch-football game with no serious injuries (but sure to leave several men limping from sore muscles). This year, the retreat committee decided not to have a speaker; instead, selected men shared their testimonies, stories of God's grace in their lives.

Greg spoke this evening about examples and role models, using his late father as an example. "Dad was my hero," Greg simply said.

An hour later, a group has casually assembled around a small campfire. At first the talk is typical of any group of men—commentary on sports, weather, and teenage sons. But someone comments on Greg's talk, and someone else asks Tony how he's doing since his father's death a week and a half ago. Tony says, "All right, I guess." He's quiet for a minute and then quietly admits his initial shock and deep grief.

After an awkward silence, the avalanche begins when Brad says, "I lost my dad three years ago, and it has been tougher than I ever thought it would be. We weren't that close, but I just can't seem to shake my feelings of sorrow, especially at certain times."

Joe jumps in. "Me too. And I got so angry. I'm still trying to figure out what happened, what's still happening, why I feel this way. I knew I'd be sad, but I thought I'd get over it and move on."

Of the ten men around the fire, seven, all those who had lost their dads, express similar thoughts and feelings. This is a big deal. They've touched a nerve.

Imagine sitting in the circle. How do you respond? What do you ask?

One year after my father died . . .

I was still angry, sad, horrified, and worried. It took a lot of talking, praying, and thinking for me to realize that I was most angry at my own mortality. If my father, whom I looked up to, had died, then certainly I would also die . . . and perhaps sooner than I surmised.

Dad died at age 77; I was 47. Suddenly, the thirty years of life I might have left seemed insufficient. I had many plans and much to experience. I was angry that death had taken my father away just as I was getting to know him as a man, and that death now was hounding my trail. I was furious that just as many aspects of my life were becoming more enjoyable and comfortable, I had to face the stark reality of my mortality.

A deep sadness lingered with me for a long time. I really missed my dad. My relationship with Dad hadn't been warm and intimate, but I was filled with so many thoughts that I wanted to share with him. I was sad that his life had to end before we could get in that last fishing trip and before he could see my children fully grown, our new home, or my growing new business. I hadn't realized how much I enjoyed updating him on all the events, victories, and defeats in my life. My mother had always been supportive, but if I could excite Dad about Erik's soccer game or Scot's new interest in business—now that would be something special.

My greatest pain came as I visualized my children attending my own funeral someday. They would have to deal with the same troubling feelings that I was experiencing. I didn't know what to do to help them.

I'm now convinced that all death is terrible. My father died as a believer in Christ, yet he experienced great indignity in dying. As a businessman, he had always dressed immaculately for work—a tie, polished shoes, knife-creased pants. But a month before his death, he had fallen, breaking his hip. He never recovered. His heart had been so weakened by congestive heart failure that surgery would have been risky. As my father declined, he lost weight; as his kidneys failed, he filled up with water.

Though his spirits were good, his body could no longer fight. The doctors agreed with our family not to prolong his life if he could not recover, but he lasted seven days after he could no longer eat or even take water intravenously! It was horrible to see Dad in that condition. Though he had always had a ready joke and a twinkle in his eye, at the end, his pain, confusion, and inability to sit, stand, or talk reduced him to a specter. As with my father, I, too, was certain of the Resurrection, but the physics of the unknown and the prospect of dying as he did frightened me greatly.

And I felt worried. How would I face a terminal illness? Would I die with serenity and dignity? Would I keep my faith knowing that I would be leaving all my loved ones behind? Was I living a healthy lifestyle to avoid these problems? Would I be able to face my children and pray with them as my father had?

My father was an exemplar for me in so many areas: sports, business, taking care of a home, personal finance, reading the Bible. And he led the way and provided a great example, even in dying.

But one year after his death, I struggled to sort out all these jumbled thoughts and painful feelings. Almost no one else could be open or patient enough to hear me out . . . unless his father had also died. (Bruce Barton)

We sat there, at his side, during his final moments: my sister, Barb, at one side of the bed and I at the other, crying, praying, stroking Dad's hair, and assuring him of our presence. Short breaths punctuated our talk and tears, with ever-increasing gaps between gasps. Then suddenly it was over . . . Dad's pain, struggle, fight for survival, and lifetime of service—seventy-two years of faithfulness.

The minutes immediately following felt unreal, almost dreamlike, as the night nurse did her work and we waited for the doctor to make his official examination and pronounce him "dead." I called my brothers, one at a time, awakening them with the news, "Dad's gone. It's over." Subdued talk followed each announcement; then tears, more talk, and whispered good-byes.

Barb and her husband, Charlie, had offered to take Dad to their home for his final days. A little more than a year earlier, we had placed Mom in the Alzheimer's wing of an eldercare facility. For the few years leading up to that day, Dad had tried to meet her needs as her caregiver. But his faithful care had broken his health. In fact, the cardiologist had informed us that Dad's heart had been irreparably damaged and was considerably weakened. The stark prognosis was that he would grow progressively weaker until the end—congestive heart failure. So we brought Dad to Chicago and took over his care, with the help of a night nurse and a hospice.

Being with Dad at death was an awesome and terrible experience . . . and a profound privilege. It was both a crisis moment and a turning point in my life. Besides the immediate trauma and deep grief, I discovered, over the subsequent months, a host of thoughts and feelings. I also learned many lessons.

Years later, I still miss my father—his engineer's logic and advice, his warm sense of humor, his concern and encouragement, and, most of all, his love. I've wanted to share my experiences and questions at each stage of life, especially marriage and parenting, and to celebrate with him my daughters' victories and accomplishments. But he's gone—Mom too—so that will have to wait. (Dave Veerman)

Such a difficult time! And in the months following the father's death, there are so many surprises. As we interviewed men, and spoke with many more, common thoughts and emotions resonated with them all. Whether they enjoyed a positive, nurturing relationship with their father or endured a destructive one, these men shared much. The following chapters will highlight these feelings and offer practical help for moving through them and on with life.

"The death of a father, yours, mine, everyone's, is traumatic, especially since it is often the first loss of a parent that a son experiences. The very man who gave us life, held us, fed us, steadied our bikes, cheered us on the field, modeled for us in the home, counseled us in our careers, and hugged us in our tears—when he dies, when we must watch him die, a part of us dies as well. No matter how well adjusted or strong we are, each son experiences the Super Bowl of grief. It is at this time when another coach and mentor is desperately needed. Someone to lead us through this most painful rite of passage."

—LEE HOUGH

We also found that many men had a difficult time at the funeral and immediately following, dealing effectively with their grief and the reality of their father's death. This can occur for any combination of the following factors.

SHOCK

For some, the death comes as an absolute shock. One man told of his father being murdered in the rest room of a hotel at a special occasion during which he was to receive an award. Another man's father died of carbon monoxide poisoning. To this day, the son doesn't know whether it was suicide or a terrible accident.

Another man was speaking at a youth camp when he learned that his father had been killed in a car crash.

In experiences such as those, surviving sons can feel numb for several days or even weeks.

EXPECTATIONS

When a person dies, we expect that person's loved ones to grieve. Often we have expectations for *how* they should grieve as well. Some of the men expressed this tension of trying to grieve in the right way.

When men don't meet those expectations, stated or implied, they can react with confusion or anger. They may think something is wrong with them because they don't have certain feelings. Or they may wonder if they really loved the person. This feeling is heightened in a son when his father dies. The young man may wonder why he can't cry, especially if he professes to having enjoyed a close relationship with his dad, and may feel as though he is going crazy.

Some, however, respond to these expectations with anger, telling others in no uncertain terms to leave them alone. They may shout something like, "You don't know how I feel!" Certainly this brings stress to other relationships. It also delays the healing process.

BUSYNESS

When a family member dies, the "man of the family" is often expected to take care of all the funeral arrangements. It's his responsibility. So when Dad dies, even if Mom is still living, the children go to work, especially the eldest son, working with the funeral director and pastor, greeting and hosting out-of-town relatives, sorting through their father's possessions and will, and so forth. In short, they find themselves not having time to grieve. They are just too busy.

"My dad was so wanting me to be a man, to grow up and, obviously, to be a godly man, but to be a man of integrity, to be a hard worker. He wanted to pass on those values. I don't know how it works. I guess I don't believe that people can look down from heaven and see the events that are happening on earth, because I guess if they could, there would be so much sadness that they would see. But I think my dad would be pleased with the man that I have become and the man that I am becoming, and I would love to have the chance to play him in Ping-Pong one more time, because he always beat me. He would gloat. He would psych you out mentally and mess with your head. Of course when you're a kid or when you're an early teen that just gets you. You don't have the experience or the wisdom to turn a deaf ear to that stuff. Even though athletically you could probably beat him, he has the mental edge. I think now if we could play, I would be less intimidated by all that stuff. Maybe in heaven I'll get to play him in Ping-Pong."

—Len Woods

Quick Return

One of the expectations faced by many men, especially from certain employers, is to return to work as soon as possible. Everyone at the plant or the office feels bad for the man and his loss, but they expect him to be back in the shop or behind his desk a day or so after the funeral. Some men take the time anyway and then have to deal with the repercussions of being gone from work. Many, however, have no say in the matter—it's out of their control.

Al returned to medical school two days after the funeral and back to the pressures of his schoolwork with no relief, no chance to think or process what happened or do anything but stay up late and study. He found this to be a very intense time. Ray K. remembers being pulled off the parade grounds at Navy boot camp to be informed of his father's death and then having to return the day after the funeral. Al and Ray had no choice. They had to return to their obligations right away.

Men who are suddenly thrust back to work or school have little opportunity to deal with all that they are feeling.

THE RIGHT THING

This phenomenon is similar to "expectations," only the man puts these expectations on himself. Many men think that they should act a certain way. For example, they may believe that they should display a tough exterior, regardless of how they feel on the inside. Others may feel pressured to express spiritual platitudes and talk about "rejoicing that Dad is in heaven," when what they really feel is anger toward God. Family custom or history can also be a determining factor in what a man thinks is "right."

These men suppress their true feelings and are shocked when those feelings burst out.

GETTING NUMB

Sadly, many men simply refuse to deal with the reality of their father's death and use alcohol or drugs to anesthetize themselves. Certainly men who already struggle in this area are more prone to respond this way. But no one is immune. Some men confess to just going out and getting drunk. When they come to themselves and their senses, they still have to face the reality that Dad is gone—they've only delayed the grief.

"For me, my father really died twice.

"I grew up without a father. Dad divorced Mom when I was two-and-a-half months old, so I didn't know him and, in fact, didn't even meet him until I was a teenager. So I went from being a toddler and knowing no father, to a young child in grade school asking questions about my father, and even into high school without knowing him. Then all of a sudden I met him. The sad part (I detail this in Choosing to Live the Blessing) *came when he said he wanted to see me play football. Our team was doing pretty well, and the local paper had a story about the team, with a picture of my twin brother and me. My father read the paper and actually called my mom and asked if he could come to the game. My brother and I played our hearts out that night, thinking he was in the stands and expecting to see him after the game. But he never showed up and never even bothered to call to say he wasn't coming. So, for me, my father died that day because I experienced the death of a dream.*

"Dad died, again, on August 6, about six years ago."

—Dr. John Trent

No Funeral

In some families, no funeral service is held. Often that means the family doesn't have the opportunity to remember the father or come to closure.

Bob, the dean of a community college, remembers that his father was opposed to funerals and memorial services. In fact, Bob's dad was reluctant to participate in any outward emotional observance. Being of English descent and Episcopalian background,

His Presence

"Today is my first Father's Day without a father. For thirty-one years I had one. I had one of the best. But now he's gone. He's buried under an oak tree in a west Texas cemetery. Even though he's gone, his presence is very near especially today.

"It seems strange that he isn't here. I guess that's because he was never gone. He was always close by. Always available. Always present. His words were nothing novel. His achievements, though admirable, were nothing extraordinary.

"But his presence was . . .

"During the turbulent years of my adolescence, Dad was one part of my life that was predictable. Girlfriends came and girlfriends went, but Dad was there. Football season turned into baseball season and turned into football season again and Dad was always there. Summer vacation, Homecoming dates, algebra, first car, driveway basketball—they all had one thing in common: his presence . . .

"Maybe that's why this Father's Day is a bit chilly. The fire has gone out. The winds of age swallowed the last splendid flame, leaving only golden embers. But there is a strange thing about those embers, stir them a bit and a flame will dance. It will dance only briefly, but it will dance. And it will knock just enough chill out of the air to remind me that he is still . . . in a special way, very present."

—MAX LUCADO. GOD CAME NEAR
(SISTERS, OREG.: MULTNOMAH PRESS, 1987), 129–31.

Bob's father feared that emotions would embarrass people in public. Though he had a great sense of humor, and he and his wife entered in at parties with great gusto, he was opposed to funerals, so he and his wife had both dedicated their bodies to medicine to be used for research or medical practice at a nearby medical school. When Bob's father died, therefore, the only service at all was held by the university in their chapel. Then they placed a plaque on the ground where his remains would eventually be buried. The plaque only had the date on it—no name. Thus, only a plate in the ground marks the grave of Bob's father, a plate with no name on it. Bob says, "Later, I went back and paid to have my parents' names added."

As a result, Bob remembers that when his father died, he wept and took a couple of long walks. He found that the lack of any service heightened his need to grieve. Having no real service made it very difficult to fully express feelings as he would have liked. He and his sister had insisted on having a small memorial service in the chapel, but Bob still felt a huge vacuum by not having a public funeral. He adds, "Without some acknowledgment of the person living and dying, grieving is incomplete." Also, with no funeral service, people from their past did not come. So he had to grieve alone.

SOUPY SPIRITUALITY

"People can make the dumbest comments at funerals," says one man. Phrases such as "God must have wanted him in heaven," or "He's in a much better place" are two of the most popular. Clichés like those fall easily from the lips of well-meaning friends and neighbors. But they have a hollow ring for the grieving person. Even if the statements are true (and certainly heaven is a "much better place" than earth), they don't bring comfort. And when repeated to a young son or daughter who has lost a parent, they can bring confusion, anger, and even a rejection of the faith. It's not unusual to hear a bitter young person say something like, "God took my dad, and I hate him for it!"

GREATER LOSS

At the time of death, Mom has the greater loss and pain. Losing a parent is difficult, but it pales in comparison to losing a spouse. So the immediate focus is on the surviving spouse. Sons may be torn between feeling bad for their moms and bad for themselves. While it's true that Mom has the biggest loss, the son feels a legitimate, significant loss as well. Sons may be so concerned for their moms that they stifle their own feelings, putting them off or considering them less significant.

SO MUCH

Finally, many find that so much is happening at one time that they can't focus on what they are feeling. One man told us that he had experienced a series of setbacks and deaths, culminating in his father's. Another shared how he had been recovering from a serious illness himself and struggling with a rebellious daughter when his father died of a heart attack. Whether grappling with personal problems, business and financial issues, interpersonal conflicts, or a combination, the accumulated effect can make it almost impossible to grieve over Dad.

A son in this situation can feel like the quarterback of a football team in the big game where suddenly both teams turn against him. He's trying to make plays, but he's surrounded.

Each of those factors merely delays coming to grips with the truth. Eventually reality hits and these sons struggle, first with their grief and then with other feelings, as the following chapters describe.

WHAT DO YOU THINK?

1. In your lifetime, what event caused you the most grief prior to the death of your father?

2. How does that compare with the loss of your father?

3. Which of the factors described above did you experience?

4. How did you respond?

5. What would you do to help someone who has experienced a tragedy such as the loss of a father?

6. What comfort have you found in Scripture?

2

THE SHOCK

Sensing the Surprisingly Wide Range and Power of Emotions

The Jensens were prepared for the worst. Dad had suffered from various ailments for several years, including a severe heart attack and quadruple bypass surgery a decade ago. Showing his age more and more with each passing year, they expected the big one would take him. Then, ironically, at 87, he had been felled by a stroke, his heart beating strong.

"He's not doing well," the doctor had said. So Craig had made the calls, and the family—Craig's sisters, brothers-in-law, nieces, and nephews—had returned. Then, gathered at the hospital, they had circled the bed and had expressed their love and prayed together, hoping that Dad, now comatose, could hear.

Death came during the night. Craig had been sleeping in a chair next to his father. At about 3:00, he awoke, and glancing at the bed thought Dad looked too still. He quickly pushed the call button, and a nurse soon appeared. A few moments later she turned to Craig and stated simply, "I'm sorry. Your father's gone."

Craig touched his father's hand and looked again at the man who had taught him to be a man. Then, after whispering "I love you, Dad," he turned and walked out the door and to the hospital elevator. It hit in the car, as he turned out of the parking lot and headed home, the first wave of grief—blinding tears and then deep, choking sobs. Craig pulled to the side of the road and wept.

"He's gone."

So final. So definite. That simple statement evokes a host of emotions and signals that life will change forever. Even when expecting Dad to die and seemingly ready, we're never *fully* prepared. After all, it's the end. So we're shocked, at first by the reality of death and its finality, and then by the depth of our grief and sense of loss.

That's how Tom E., a director of development at a college in Indiana, felt. "The finality of it! My dad's gone; the chapter's closed. I immediately thought of the loss of his prayer, counsel, wisdom, birthday cards," he recalls. "It certainly helped me understand the brevity of life."

Art, a church denominational executive, was 47 when his father died at the age of 67. Art and his dad were especially close. In his words, "On a scale of 1 to 10 (with 10 being great) our relationship was a 15." Art admits that soon after his father's death he would talk to pictures of his dad hanging on the wall, as though they were having a conversation. He also locked himself in a room and listened to one of his dad's favorite CDs while drinking a bottle of wine his dad had made. "All the while I just kept saying, 'Dad' out loud, over and over."

"I felt a sense of great loss," recalls Mark S., a publisher from Nashville. "It hit me hard as I thought of the tremendous impact my father had upon my life, more than any other person—and now he was gone. The one who had shaped and molded me was no longer there for me."

Todd, a project manager for an electric utility, was 36 when his father died of a heart attack while taking a nap. He was 63. Todd found it difficult to sleep for a couple of weeks. And he adds, "I cried the whole week following Dad's death. My brother came home and took care of everything so I could mourn. I just let my guard down and didn't care what people thought—it really poured out."

IMMEDIATE RESPONSE

For men like Craig and Todd, grief flows freely, with streaming tears and gut-wrenching sobs. Others show stoic resolve, keeping their feelings inside. Some seek the comfort of loved ones, while others pull away to work it out silently, in private. Each person deals uniquely with the emotions of the moment.

Most men feel awkward at outbursts of grief, especially their own. We've been conditioned, and even taught, to suppress our tears and fears, to keep those emotions in check, inside. We're supposed to suck it up and be a man! Our fathers modeled that style. They knew their job and their place, and, with John Wayne bravado, they did what had to be done. They were tough guys, doers, builders, warriors. Thus our feelings catch us off guard at that terrible moment. Those we interviewed, in particular those who were adults when their fathers died, revealed their surprise and even shock at the depth of their emotional responses.

That was the experience of Bill W., a business owner and an ordained minister. He says, "What surprised me first was my dad's reaction when he learned he was dying. Dad was not one to show emotion. In fact, he had hit the beach at D-day but had never spoken of that experience. He bore physical and emotional scars from the war but never opened up. Later, I found his discharge papers and his two Purple Hearts. Yet as he lay dying, he broke down. I was also surprised at the emotional toll on me, especially being a guy. I had time to prepare, but I lost it too. Later, I went to his grave, sat down, and wept."

Often the grief is mixed with anger; or, expecting grief, men get angry instead. Sometimes the anger is directed at God but usually at the situation, at the reality of what has occurred and that death has to come at all. Many men are able to express anger more easily than sorrow.

Anger was part of John D.'s response. John, a music educator and father of three, was 40 and his father was 73. John's father had been experiencing intense abdominal pain that would suddenly hit and then recede. The symptoms hadn't been properly diagnosed, however, so his hospitalization came too late—he bled to death internally. John says, "I was a wreck. I was not prepared. My kids wondered if I was going to be OK. At the time I felt anger toward God for taking him, and, for a while after that, anger at the hospital for their slow response."

Jim G., a business consultant, was 30 when his father died suddenly of a heart attack at 56, a relatively young man. Jim's first response was anger. He says, "I knew the other stages of grieving and *expected* them, but I wasn't prepared for the anger and depression. I was angry. People ticked me off. My temper was on a short fuse, and I would get mad over little things. Then came the depression. I had gone through the funeral, had understood what had happened, and had processed it. I didn't feel down. Then, about a week and a half later, I was mowing the grass, and the lawnmower was getting heavier and heavier. About halfway through, I could barely push it. We don't have any hills, but I could barely push the mower across the front yard. I was depressed. I wasn't *feeling* depressed, but my energy was down to nothing."

Many who knew they would be sad were shocked at the depth of their sadness. Others were surprised at the opposite response— their *lack* of emotion. When hit with the news, they merely felt empty and numb. Then they felt guilty for *not* being sad.

A writer and minister from Louisiana, Len was just a teenager when he lost his dad to cancer. "I sobbed the day we learned of Dad's illness," Len recalls. "Then the day he died, I never shed a tear, nor at the funeral. I think emotionally I just shut down for a long time. In retrospect, it's scary that a person could be so closed off. I don't think it's healthy, and I wouldn't counsel anyone to do that. Maybe it was my age, or maybe it was that plus the kind of nonemotional relationship my father and I had. My lack of emotion certainly caught me by surprise."

When Bill W.'s father died, he felt a sense of relief because of the years he had spent dealing with his dad's alcoholism and failing health. Bill says, "It had been so hard with him that I don't remember crying. Then I felt guilty for not crying."

Certainly a person will grieve at any loss, especially the death of a loved one. And next to the loss of a child or wife, there's no comparison. That's not the point—it's not a matter of scale. Instead, what seems to shock men the most is that *this* loss is felt so deeply. Even men who were estranged from their fathers and those who had months and even years to prepare express their surprise. Why? What makes this loss unique and so devastating? In our discussions with counselors and other professionals and in our interviews, several revealing aspects emerged.

FIRST REAL LOSS

For many, the father is the first person in the immediate family to die. This may seem obvious in light of well-known mortality statistics. Simply summarized, old people tend to die before young people, and men tend to die sooner than women. Certainly, many exceptions to those statements can be found. But a vast majority of people would say that the first funeral they remember attending, as a kid, was for "Grandpa." Is that the way it was for you?

Now, fast-forward a few years—what was the first funeral that your children experienced? Again, it was probably *their* grandfather. And when that loved one is also *your* father, it hits home, big time.

Many can say with Spike, "Dad was the first one close to me to die. It was a shock!"

"Make no mistake about it—the death of a father causes a very significant wound! Some of us tend the wound; some of us ignore it. But, surprisingly, the wound is not that our father died and by his death our world is forever altered or changed. No, the wound is that the world around us acknowledged the death for one brief moment and then skipped merrily on its way. The death of our father! An event of such consequence to us! And yet soon, too soon, even those near and dear to us forgot. They stopped saying, 'Sorry to hear about your dad,' or 'How's your mom adjusting?' Or especially, 'How's it going with you?' The wound of apathy, of indifference—that's the truly significant wound."

—HAROLD IVAN SMITH. ON GRIEVING THE DEATH OF A FATHER (MINNEAPOLIS, MINN.: AUGSBURG FORTRESS, 1994), 12.

BIGGER THAN LIFE

We can laugh now at playground taunts of "My dad's tougher than your dad!" But many of us lived out those interactions and sincerely believed as we were growing up that our fathers were the biggest and strongest—invincible. When we were little boys, our dads certainly were bigger and stronger than we were, and many of us grew up thinking they could do just about anything. Older siblings may remember Dad playing softball on the church team, shooting hoops at the park, digging holes for fence posts, or putting a new roof on the house. Even if a father wasn't a strong physical specimen, he was smart. To his children, Dad knows everything and has all the answers.

We find it hard to believe that anything could hurt him or slow him down. So when tragedy strikes, we reel in disbelief. We may think we have outgrown the idea that Dad is invincible. Our reaction to his death, however, reveals that we have hung on to that idea well into adulthood.

"I was numb by the time Dad died. Our family had been to see him in the hospital several times. He was in for five weeks until he passed away. Each visit seemed like the last we would see him. That year held so many shocks and changes, and they were piling up. Dad was dying; my daughter, our firstborn, was leaving for college; I had just left a ministry where I had served for twenty-six years; two friends and I were starting a new business; I had moved into a new home; I was the negotiator in a tough church split. During this time, I felt that if I gave in to my emotions, all my strength would fly out like a released balloon."

—BRUCE BARTON

"My dad served in World War II, in the Navy, in the Pacific Theater as the commander of a little LST. Later, he started a construction business that was very successful," explains Len. "Dad made me feel safe. I felt provided for. I felt like he would be there for us. I remember playing basketball, and he'd come home from work and would say, 'Give me the ball—give me the ball.' Then he'd grab it and shoot it. So when we found out he was sick, that he had cancer, I was confused. How could someone so strong and healthy be so sick?"

Mateen, a pastor in Illinois, says, "Unless they've been infirm for a long, long time, you tend not to think of your parents, especially your father, as someone who is subject to death or getting feeble. I think it's always a surprise when a father dies when he hasn't been battling physical problems for a long time. So I was shocked to learn that my dad had died, even though we all knew that with congestive heart failure, sooner or later his heart would get too tired to keep going."

Jeff R., a high-school athletic director, relates, "Dad was my hero and still is. He spent a ton of time with me as a boy and was a great dad. We did everything together: games, church, on the farm. At 56 he was diagnosed with leukemia, and he died thirteen years later—I was at his side. That was the most difficult blessing I ever had." When the father is the son's "hero," as with Jeff, he assumes almost mythic proportions. The son can't imagine anything bad ever happening to Dad.

Mike S., a college football coach, also describes his father as his hero. He explains, "Dad was also my final authority—I could always get an answer. I never left any conversation wondering what his opinion was. He was a tough guy, too, a typical WWII throwback." Mike's father fought cancer with that toughness for the last two years of his life. Mike adds, "Up until the last couple of days, I denied the reality of his condition. I figured he'd win at this, like he did at everything else."

> *"Much like a mighty tree, my dad's true colors were the most vivid at the end of his life. When he had just hours left to live, I truly saw my father at his brightest, clearest, and finest. It was a day I will never forget."*
>
> —JOHN ASHCROFT. LESSONS FROM A FATHER TO HIS SON (NASHVILLE, TENN.: THOMAS NELSON PUBLISHERS, 1998), 195.

PAINFUL FLASHBACKS

Another reason men feel the loss of their father so deeply can be the emotional memory of previous pain.

Dr. Ken Canfield, the founder of the National Center for Fathering, has spent a lifetime studying men—their attitudes, beliefs, actions, and reactions. He asserts that losing a father can bring to the forefront all the grief a man has suffered over the years, including, even, the loss of a baby during pregnancy. During that terrible time for a couple, the man usually tries to be strong for his wife, reassuring and comforting. As a result, he often stuffs his own grief and goes back to work.

Years later when his father dies, however, it comes crashing in—the intense pain of that loss and several others. This man misses his dad, but his tears flow from a much deeper place.

GUILT

In addition, the grief of many men is exacerbated by the realization that time has run out to right past wrongs. Resolving conflicts and taking back words spoken in haste are not possible. Regardless of who or what caused the breach in the relationship, a son who has unfinished business with his father will often have an intense reaction at his father's death.

That's what happened to Jerry H., an attorney from Georgia. He explains, "My father had been ill for several years following a massive stroke. The year prior to his stroke, after a lengthy conversation at his office, he told me uncategorically in the most straightforward of ways, 'Your life has been a total disappointment.'

"'To who, Dad—you or me?' I responded. With that comment I walked out of his office and virtually out of his life. I saw him at family get-togethers, yet a distance existed that could not be bridged. I was well prepared for my father's demise, having dealt with his illness and the family turmoil that comes when the 'leader' upon whom so many rely falls. What I was not prepared for, though, was the effect of having so much left open, unresolved, and hanging in our relationship."

Unresolved conflict with a deceased father may then lead to anger ("How could he do this to me and die?"), guilt ("It's my fault"), and depression ("Now I'll never be able to make it right").

REGRETS

This is another powerful contributing factor. Even when the relationship has been positive, with no unresolved conflicts or major issues, regret can intrude. This often occurs when death comes sooner than expected. The son didn't have time to say good-bye, to have that heart-to-heart talk he had been putting off, to get the finances in order, or to say "I love you" one last time.

"Your father's death shapes you regardless of the status of your relationship with him at the time of his death. In ways apparent and not so apparent, his death shapes you."

—HAROLD IVAN SMITH. ON GRIEVING THE DEATH OF A FATHER (MINNEAPOLIS, MINN.: AUGSBURG FORTRESS, 1994), 13.

Roger, a youth ministry executive from Colorado, describes his relationship with his father as "nice, but never got real deep." He adds, "Dad's generation didn't talk about their feelings—they barreled through life."

Roger's father's health had not been good. But when he received the call that his father had been taken to the hospital, he wasn't told the severity of his father's condition—there had been other hospital stays—so Roger decided not to make the trip home. Soon after, Roger's brother called and explained the seriousness of the situation. He said there was nothing that Roger could do.

Roger reflects, "I felt so frustrated and powerless. And my biggest regret was that I didn't have the chance to say good-bye to Dad. In fact, things happened so fast that I never really had a time to grieve until a week or two after the funeral. Later I visited a counselor who, during our time together, suggested that I speak to the empty chair next to me, pretending that my father was sitting there. I turned toward the chair and began to talk. I felt foolish at first, but as I expressed myself to 'Dad' and said my good-byes, the tears began to flow. It was very therapeutic."

Reflecting on his experience, Jeff B., an Illinois businessman, says, "If I had known my father was going to die so soon, I would have expressed even more of my thoughts and feelings with him. I would have been very specific. I wish he could have heard all the things I said to other people about him."

Regrets can also include second-guessing, thinking about what might have been or should have been. "I had many thoughts about my dad after he died," says Phil V., a business executive in the Twin Cities, "thoughts of what my dad could have done to not have a heart attack—eat better, proper exercise? Thoughts about his faith and his relationship with Mom. Thoughts about myself and whether I should have moved so far away from my folks."

Jim W., a college professor in Illinois, admits that he and his father weren't very close—they didn't talk much. Jim's dad was a hard worker who spent most of each day on the job. But as a government employee, he couldn't discuss his work. Jim says, "When my father died, I was saddened thinking that if he had lived longer, we would have spent some time together. I regret not doing that." Jim's father was 73 when he died.

"I was startled to find Patty in the waiting room one Monday morning. Visitors are never allowed inside the compound until four o'clock. The look of sorrow in her eyes forewarned me.

"'It's Dad, isn't it?' I asked.

"'Yes, Chuck, but he went very peacefully—this morning.'

"I held her tight, fighting my emotions. She knew how close my father and I had been. A hundred thoughts tumbled through my mind at that moment. Grief that he was gone, gratitude that it had been peaceful and painless. Memories of the last time I saw him, when he was in the hospital and we talked about my pleading guilty. Concern for my mother, now all alone. But overall a deep remorse that my dad had left this world knowing that his only son was in prison. What a sharp contrast to that proud moment when he had listened to the President praise his Special Counsel."

—CHUCK COLSON. BORN AGAIN (LINCOLN, VA.: CHOSEN BOOKS, 1976), 261.

LOSS OF SELF

One of the strongest emotion-producers is also the most difficult to pin down—the identity factor. A man identifies so strongly with his father that when his father dies, the son feels as though part of him has died as well. A family may have three sons, each one a unique individual with God-given abilities and personality. Yet each one will be like his dad.

Paul V., a development director from Connecticut, sees his personality reflecting his father's. He says, "I wish I hadn't learned to keep my emotions to myself so well. I believe that was from Dad, and I learned it."

Check out your values—you caught them from your parents (we'll discuss this later). Or think of the interests you shared with your father. You both may have enjoyed music or sports or telling jokes or discussing politics.

We even begin to look like him. How often have you heard, "You look just like your father"? The family resemblance marks us. Whether by heredity or environment or both, we're connected. Thus, many sons feel as though part of themselves died with their dads.

> *"Grief is a gradual, uneven, and lengthy process, since it involves, in a very real sense, the loss of part of oneself, that aspect of one's personality that was uniquely drawn out of a person in the presence of his father."*
>
> —Dr. Ken Boa

Dick E., a stewardship executive for a Christian college, explains that he always tried to measure up to his father's expectations and standards. He recalls working one summer for his father's (nicknamed "Red") construction crew: "I never worked so hard, labor-wise. Down in holes shoveling slag. But the one thing that really motivated me was that the other workers would say that I was Red's boy—that demanded that I work extra hard. I think it's part of who I am. But what it really came down to was measuring up to what he would want me to do." Dick was only 30 when his father died, at 55, in a car accident. Now that Dick has surpassed his father's age, he sees that he even resembles his father physically. He says, "My wife says I'm more like him than I ever thought I was."

Ralph, a management consultant in Orlando, remembers, "I had always felt very close to Dad. And his last couple of years, we

"The lives of fathers and sons are intertwined; when one dies, the other is diminished."

—JOHN ASHCROFT. *LESSONS FROM A FATHER TO HIS SON* (NASHVILLE, TENN.: THOMAS NELSON PUBLISHERS, 1998), 218.

had a sense of bonding. He had lost Mom through Alzheimer's, and I had lost my wife through divorce. We both felt so lonely, and we shared a fellowship of suffering. When I heard he was gone, I cried myself to sleep . . . for two or three nights . . . and I remember picturing myself hanging onto the cross and praying, 'Dad's gone—you're all I have, God.' I was surprised by how profoundly I missed Dad. He was my buddy. I felt as though I had a hole in my heart."

Jeff B. uses that same expression: "It leaves a hole in your heart. And it was a bigger piece than I thought it would be."

Any combination of these factors will intensify the emotions. It's no wonder that men are blindsided by their feelings—shocked at the depth of their grief. Many refer to the experience as pivotal or life-changing.

But this immediate response is just the beginning.

WHAT DO YOU THINK?

1. What do you remember grieving over as a child?

2. What is the first funeral that you remember? How did you feel?

3. With whom did you first share your grief over losing your dad?

4. With whom was it most difficult to show sadness and tears?

5. Who helped you the most in the first few weeks following your father's death? What was the most helpful advice you received?

6. Initially, what was the most difficult aspect of dealing with your father's death?

7. What regrets do you have about your relationship with your father?

8. How do you normally express your grief?

9. What physical effects did you experience as a result of your father's death and your grief the first few weeks after he died (for example, fatigue, numbness, anger, etc.)?

3

AFTERSHOCKS
Experiencing Emotional Waves

An earthquake has devastating effects. Highways buckle, pipes burst, buildings crumble, and huge fissures suddenly appear. Surprised victims feel stunned, tossed, and battered both physically and emotionally. Then the aftershocks roll in over the next few days and weeks, robbing victims of sleep and heightening their sense of insecurity and anxiety.

The death of a father has similar shocking and debilitating effects on a son. It shakes a man to his core. And the depth of the grief he experiences can be shocking and baffling to him. Yet the aftershocks can be even more traumatic, as reactions invade months, years, and even decades after the death.

We men have experienced loss before. As a child, when our pet died, we cried bitterly—but the sorrow subsided, and soon we were back to normal . . . and our parents bought a new pet. A few years later, when we returned home from camp and broke off the summer romance, we sulked and brooded for two weeks—but school began, and we moved on. Then, junior year, the other team sank a shot at the buzzer, knocking us out of the tournament. With faces contorted in disbelief we mourned with our teammates—but soon we faced another season and new games. And when "the love of our life" dumped us and we thought we'd never love again, we did.

Through the years, we faced each disappointment and heartache, grieved, and got over it. When confronted with tough times, we made it through. We men are problem-solvers; we find a way. We size up the situation and say, "Show me the tools of the trade and the rules of the game—I'll make it!"

But a father's death is different—the tools don't work, and the rules don't apply. Men told us that they thought the process would be the same, that time would heal the wound, even one this deep. Seemingly out of nowhere, however, feelings of sorrow, despair, or rage returned, and they grieved again. Even if they had released great emotion at the time of the father's death, aftershocks of sorrow rolled through their lives.

- Paul L., a ministry executive from Atlanta, says, "I am surprised that I am shedding tears right now as I discuss memories of my dad three months after his death."

- According to Jeff B., "I thought I was ready for Dad's death and had grieved his loss. But as the years have gone along, I've missed him more. I would never have expected it."

- Todd adds, "Thoughts of Dad can make me stop what I am doing and cry."

- Al, a physician in Arizona, describes being surprised "that the memories and feelings came back slowly, not all at once."

OUT OF THE BLUE

These waves of memories and emotions can hit suddenly, without warning. The man who was close to his father will grieve because he misses his dad, especially at those times when they would have celebrated together, shared a meal, or talked things over. Or perhaps a tune, a date on the calendar, a distinctive smell, or a place will evoke the feelings.

- "The emotions came off and on, and I was totally unprepared," John D. explains. "I was surprised to learn how fragile I was and the depth of the love I had for Dad. Weeks after the death, during a stressful time, I'd be driving and it would hit, and I'd start crying. On holidays and August 10, the anniversary of his death, I would miss him the most."

- Ty, an associate dean of students at an Indiana college, says, "A song, a phrase, or a specific memory will trigger a sense of loss."

- "Whenever I smell a cigar or see a hard hat, that's my dad. That's the image," says Dick E. "I remember my father and feel the loss again."

Many of the men we interviewed would tear up or take a personal moment and cry as we talked, sometimes even decades after losing their dads. The discussion would stir up strong memories and emotions.

Dick E. adds, "Even when I get my emotions under control, they're not under control. To talk about these things thirty years later—it could be ten years more from now—I'll still do the same thing. I'll still feel the same turmoil inside. So letting it out is something that I just feel like, 'man I don't want to go there again.' I don't know how I'll be with the death of other loved ones, but I don't think it will be the same. I'm not sure why."

"I wish I had known how to handle the immense sadness," says Tom L., a teacher from Illinois. "I dealt with it by keeping busy. I was coaching three sports, teaching, and rearing a family, so I immersed myself in those activities." Then Tom adds, "I would find myself missing my father so much at times. In fact, I would just start to cry several months later, usually when I was doing some menial task that took no thought, like mowing the lawn. My thoughts would turn to Dad."

"I was surprised by the random surfacing of sorrow."

—MAX LUCADO

The emotions come up from deep within us. They will break through somewhere. It won't always be logical or when the man expects. They find the weakest point in his shell to break through.

A DEEP LONGING

Men who struggled in relating with their fathers or who had absent, alcoholic, or even abusive fathers also experience the aftershocks. But they grieve for what might have been or should have been. Again, these tears flow unexpectedly, at unpredictable moments.

In this regard, Bill J., a pastor in San Diego, tells of seeing the movie *Field of Dreams*. He explains, "At the end of the movie, the son says, 'Dad, you want to have a catch?' When I heard that, I bawled like a baby. I was saddened by realizing what I never had, and I wondered what it would have been like to have known my father as a young man before he became beaten down by life."

Dr. John Trent, a well-known counselor and writer, shares: "My father was a World War II veteran who couldn't get over fighting the war. He was an angry alcoholic, suffering flashbacks and hurt—all the trauma of war. He really never recovered—he was a mess. In a sense, therefore, when I first met my dad, my dream died—my idealistic dream that my father would put his arm around me and then suddenly all those years of lost memories would be forgotten with a great guy who was taken with me. Well, that didn't happen.

"After I became a Christian, I worked very hard to build a relationship with my father. Before that I hated him. Even afterward I just intensely disliked him, and I relabeled the emotion since I couldn't hate him anymore as a Christian. Only years later was I finally able to forgive my father and realize why he never blessed my brother or me or encouraged us. He had never been 'blessed' by his father, so he was just passing down to us what he never received.

"Over the years, I worked hard to build a relationship with my father. He was dying basically destitute, and I had paid for him to be in three different nursing homes. Eventually, I had him convalesce in our home for six weeks thinking that somehow that would build a relationship between us, but it never happened. I'm a good question asker. I'm a counselor. I'm paid to ask questions. Yet I could never get my father to really open up. So going into that last day with my father I thought and felt, *Maybe this will be the day that he really opens up.* It never happened, and he died of congestive heart and lung failure. The last few hours as I held his hand and as he coughed his life away, I heard no words of love or forgiveness or affirmation or encouragement.

"When my dad died, I felt a tremendous sense of loss. For men, like me, who have grown up without a father, when he dies it's almost like losing an uncle, not a father. I was trying so hard to connect, and then he died and I suddenly realized that it was over. When my father breathed his last, I literally sensed his spirit leaving. The instant he took his last breath, his body went from life to just matter. It was incredible. And with the tears came a deep sense of knowing that in this lifetime I would never get my dad's blessing. That's true for many men. They have a huge sense that now it will never happen."

Dave, a sales executive in Illinois, was 12 and the youngest of three brothers when his father died from the effects of alcoholism. (His father was 46.) Dave says, "I knew my father wasn't doing well, but I thought he would go through rehab and be OK. When he died, I was in shock, disbelief. And I was afraid, wondering what would happen now. I was very emotional. But I got over it, I thought. Then about eighteen years later, I went to a seminar at church. It was about being a better father. When I heard all those men sharing their good times with their dads, I began to get angry and left in the middle of the seminar. I hadn't had that kind of relationship with my father, and I had a feeling of emptiness and loss, that I had been shortchanged. I totally broke down on the way home.

"When I got there, my wife saw that I was upset and said, 'What happened to you?' Then she suggested that I go to a counselor. I didn't want to—I even told the guy I didn't believe in counseling and thought it was a waste of time. But we met every two weeks for a year, and he helped me understand my feelings. I cried in every other session, all year. I also returned to the cemetery; there I discovered that my father didn't have a headstone. Evidently we hadn't been able to afford one. So I had one made. Then I held my own funeral for Dad."

Dave's older brother, Bill, owner of a building rehab company in Chicago, describes his relationship with his father this way: "I really didn't have one except that he was my father. He was very introverted and didn't do anything with us boys. He just worked at the family gas station. We would see him on Sundays when we'd watch Art Linkletter and Disney on TV and make pizzas together. He made a good pizza." Bill says that when he got the call about his father dying (Bill was 13 at the time), he went to church, walked to the altar, and cried. A few years later, Bill was playing catch with a friend. He says, "It hit me. I never played ball with my dad!" He adds, "Every year on the anniversary of his death, in October, it's a blue time for me."

A Good Cry

"If I weren't sitting in a major airport right now, I think I would have a good cry.

"But society says no to that behavior. And my dad was part of that society. He taught me, 'Big boys don't cry.' He discounted my protests: 'But, Daddy, it hurts!'

"If my sister were here, she could cry, and no one would say a thing. My heartbreak is just as severe, and I am supposed to sit here and take it 'like a man.'

"Right at this moment, I don't want to be a man. I want some relief from this ache inside. No wonder grown men have aches and pains that physicians cannot find.

"Dad always said after he had punished me, 'Quit crying, or I'll give you something to cry about!'

"Dad, you did just that. By dying."

—HAROLD IVAN SMITH. ON GRIEVING THE DEATH OF A FATHER (MINNEAPOLIS, MINN.: AUGSBURG FORTRESS, 1994), 78.

The oldest of the three brothers, Ray K., a professional counselor, shares, "Dad never went to any of my gymnastic meets. He was in town but never came. He was a nice guy but never there. I remember, when I was four, building an airplane out of a cardboard box. I told Mom that I wanted to fly and see my dad."

Ray continues, "I was 18 and in Navy boot camp when I got the word. We were drilling, and a Red Cross person pulled me out. Right after the funeral, I had to return, so I didn't have the chance to mourn. Then, when I got out of the Navy two years later, I started college. During that time, I was in therapy with a counselor for two and a half years, and I wept and wept and wept. He helped me get in touch with my profound sense of loss. This is what led me to become a therapist."

Phil M.'s dad had a long fight with lung cancer, a fight that everyone thought was successful. His father was ready to return to work when the doctors discovered that he had brain cancer too. He died a few months later at age 50. Phil was 13. He remembers, "For two days after my father died I didn't shed a tear. In fact, I didn't really cry until after the funeral, and then I couldn't stop for about half an hour. After that, I curled up inside myself and tried not to show emotion about anything. But now I always get teary when I think of him—probably once or twice a week. I know there's a lot of pain, and it has to be worked through."

Len, who was in high school when his father died, shed few tears at the funeral. He says, "You can't keep the emotions in check forever. They will leak out somewhere. And God used movies with me, interestingly enough. In many films, the plot or one of the subplots involves a relationship between a father and a son—*Legends of the Fall*, *Dad*, and *A River Runs Through It* are a few. Movies like that make me cry because I think of what I missed with my father."

Too Busy for Grief

The death pulled some men abruptly from a chaotic schedule and thrust them into a whirlwind of funeral arrangements. Only later, then, did the full reality of their father's death sink in. They were too busy to grieve.

Ray mentioned that he left boot camp and was quickly in and out of town for the funeral. Other men remember being numb or stunned at the funeral or being busily engaged in greeting out-of-town relatives, friends, and other mourners and well-wishers.

I had worked for my dad in the summers, so I knew his friends from work. They all came. And then there were all the relatives. I couldn't really deal with what I was feeling. I was doing my best to talk with everyone, as though I was the host. (Bruce Barton)

Jim G. remembers, "Dad's passing was sudden, and the time at the funeral home was scheduled very quickly, like two days later. It was packed with all kinds of people from the community and his work. I had to greet all my relatives and take care of Mom. There were so many people to catch up with and talk to, from every aspect of our lives."

If a son is young when his father dies, he may feel overwhelmed by the number of people at the funeral and by all the attention. Only later, when everyone has left and the boy is alone with the rest of the family, without Dad, will the reality of his father's death begin to sink in.

Though many men remembered very little of the funeral service itself, they were helped by the gathering of family and friends around them. Others found great comfort in the words of the Christian funeral service.

I called the pastor to get all the Scripture references that he had read at the funeral. At the time I had not been able to absorb them, but I wanted them to sink in.

I knew my father believed in Christ, but my faith was nagging me. I had attended a Christian college and theological seminary and had worked in youth ministry for nearly three decades. I knew the Bible. But the reality of the resurrection of my dad's body and my body was tough to accept. Was my faith weak? Was the stark reality of death threatening me? Was I afraid of death or just the unknown? I tend to be skeptical, and my mind can't grasp how it all works. So I wondered how

The first poem of "Memorial Quartet" Francis A. Noll, November 6, 1918– January 6, 1993 (to my own son David)

At Calvary Baptist there has always been
a men's quartet, and so there was the night
of January ninth when once again
above the flood of words a song took flight
of faith from Henry, Terry, Wayne, and Dale.
Then high and fine Luane sang tenderly
to ask if souls were well when in a gale
the sorrows rolled like billows of the sea.
And now, months past, if still the sorrows roll
despite what we believe about the sting
of death, it must be for the gaping hole
he left who, even if his ear was tin,
so loved to hear the men of Calvary sing
their songs of Jesus' triumph over sin.

—DR. MARK A. NOLL. SEASONS OF GRACE (GRAND RAPIDS, MICH.: BAKER BOOK HOUSE, 1997), 62.

molecules could be gathered from all over the earth and how mortified bodies could be reconstituted into a living person. Was my father really healed, body and soul, memories and emotions? Was he really welcomed into heaven by his mother and father? And I prayed,

"Lord, please let it be true . . . and also for me."

So I struggled to accept this great miracle and work of God. I carried with me the verses from the funeral service like a valuable treasure. I reviewed them and prayed them many times.

I know Jesus loves me and that he died for me. During those days, however, my mind wouldn't trust the words, and my body wouldn't rest in the promise. The only way I could deal with these feelings was to take Jesus' words as spoken to me: "There are many rooms in my Father's home, and I am going to prepare a place for you. If this were not so, I would tell you plainly" (John 14:2). (Bruce Barton)

IN OUR DREAMS

For many sons, the grief process involves dreams. Freud asserted that dreams are wish fulfillment. If that is true, then it explains why the father is alive and everyone is happy in the dreams.

Every now and then I will dream that Dad is alive. In the dream, we're talking or working together or watching my daughters play a sport or perform. When I awake, I always feel sad knowing that it wasn't real. I can't ever remember what Dad and I discussed in the dream—I just remember it being an important conversation. (Dave Veerman)

Tom T., an investment counselor, was in his midthirties when his father committed suicide. Tom says that he hadn't had much of a relationship with his father for several years. Tom explains that when he got the news, "I had some sense of loss but not a deep sense of grief because I didn't have the depth of emotional relationship at that point. If anything bothered me, it was the lack of grief." He adds, "I can remember for two or three years having dreams in which I would see my father somewhere. I would be walking down the street, and I would see him. So obviously there was a sense of loss because I was having those dreams. It was buried subconsciously."

Dreams of his father also became part of Jim G.'s story. He says, "I had a dream once, a couple of months after my father died, still wanting my dad to come back and sort of finish off, stay around till retirement and say good-bye to people and all those kind of things. In the dream he was alive again, sitting at the kitchen table, not saying anything but just smiling as he normally did."

Harry, a telecommunications executive from Illinois, admits that even to this day he dreams about his dad. (His father died seventeen years ago.) In these dreams, his father is alive, and they are doing things together. "I always wake up feeling good about having been with him again," he says. But then he gets emotional as he remembers that he missed arriving at the hospital in time to say good-bye to his father. (He had to fly back from out East.)

DIFFERENCES

Every person is a unique creation of God with a distinctive personal history, personality, mix of talents and gifts, and style. Any generalizations about human behavior, therefore, will stand on shaky ground. Different people respond differently to virtually the same set of circumstances, including the death of a loved one. In general, however, we found that men were *surprised* by their emotional reactions following their father's death. For most, the event was much bigger than anticipated.

In addition, recent studies reveal that men, generally speaking, grieve differently than women. Most women, it seems, tend to let everything out and let it flow, freely expressing their sorrow. In contrast, many men, as we have already seen, keep their feelings in check or hide them, only to see those feelings surface in the future. And even those whose feelings come

> *"Grief is a long process with unexpected twists."*
>
> —DR. KEN BOA

out right away find themselves continuing to deal with their loss, months and even years later.

According to Elizabeth Levang in *When Men Grieve*, "The sexes have very different languages for grief. The ways they process their emotions are unique too. Men tend to *think* their way through grief; their intellect is their guide. Women seem to *feel* their way through grief; emotion is their pilot."[1] Thus, as we have seen, men may think they have resolved the issue and have finished grieving and then are shocked when the feelings resurface.

"Remembrances of a father after these moments catch the griever by surprise. Recently I noticed my father's watch in a dark corner of my safety deposit box. Its presence there exemplified the great value I had assigned it. As I turned the watch in my hand, I remembered my father's commitment to being on time, always, if not early."

—HAROLD IVAN SMITH. ON GRIEVING THE DEATH OF A FATHER (MINNEAPOLIS, MINN: AUGSBURG FORTRESS, 1994), 13.

Neil Chethik writes, "In recent decades, psychologists and grief counselors have tended to consider crying and talking—the traditionally female style of mourning—as the gold standard for grieving . . . As a result, well-meaning therapists, spouses, partners, and friends have sometimes tried to steer a bereaved man toward his tears. And for some men, it's been effective. Their mourning process is eruptive, not unlike a volcano, tears flowing like hot lava, releasing the pressure beneath. However, most men in my research seemed to mourn in more subtle ways. Their emotions moved more like tectonic plates, shifting far below the surface, sending out tremors and shudders, perhaps the occasional tear. And the aftershocks often went on for years."[2] Thus, as we have heard from many men, the tears return at unexpected moments.

Some men found themselves reacting to their fathers' deaths with anger, again, even months and years later. For example, Jerry W. explains, "Over the years, I had an anger at God because I didn't get what I wanted. I didn't think God was there for me. And I was angry with God because I thought he took away my father's life. And I was angry at my father for abandoning me."

Phil V. says, "I was angry because I thought Dad should have and could have lived longer."

According to Dr. Levang, "Anger is [men's] protest against a past that is forever lost, a present that can never be restored, and a future that will never be."[3]

Oliver, a college professor in Tennessee, was 45 when his father died at age 69. He describes his emotional reaction as delayed rage. "I remember when I heard the news of my father's death and when I went to the funeral, I never cried once in any of that time. My father died in January, and my birthday is March 10. I went to bed the night of my birthday, but I woke up screaming in the middle of the night. I kept screaming, 'My father's dead! My father's dead!' I know this is the adult equivalent of, 'I want my daddy,' but that's what I heard myself saying. That shocked me. I guess I was thinking that after all this time you kind of move on. But I would have to say there probably isn't a day that goes by that I don't think about these things."

Oliver continues, "Rage would emerge in a way that I don't think I ever had experienced before. Unfortunately, sometimes my wife and kids caught the brunt of it. I started saying things that I really had not said since I had become a Christian. In twenty years I had not talked this way. So why all of a sudden did I start saying those things? I wondered. My wife has been a tremendous help—it's amazing she hasn't left me."

"Men are taught to be less self-disclosing, less expressive, and less interdependent. Women, on the other hand, are encouraged to focus on affiliation, connectedness, and intimacy. Women not only desire expressiveness, they need to express their feelings. Men's inexpressive tendencies cause conflict. It is as if the genders are at cross-purposes."

—ELIZABETH LEVANG. WHEN MEN GRIEVE (MINNEAPOLIS, MINN.: FAIRVIEW PRESS, 1998), 41.

POTENTIAL MISUNDERSTANDING

This contrast in mourning styles can lead to misunderstanding between men and women. Some women will cry more at the father-in-law's funeral than the husband and wonder how he can be so stoic and calm. Later, many of those wives who grieved deeply and then moved on may lose patience with husbands who mourn, months and years afterward. In an argument, a wife may even challenge the husband's manhood with statements like, "Grow up! Deal with it!" or mock him for his emotional fragility and vulnerability. She just can't see why it's such a big deal, especially considering what she has experienced in life.

When Mateen became a Christian, his father was shocked, even scandalized. As a Muslim living in Saudi Arabia, he could not accept that his son had become a follower of Christ and, even more disturbing, a seminary student. Mateen says, "When I was 20, my dad and I had a pretty vibrant relationship. Then it all screeched to a halt when I became a Christian. He effectively wrote me out of his life and out of the family." Over the years, father and son were reconciled somewhat, but the relationship never became close again. When Mateen left Arabia to return to college, he thought it would be the last time he would see his parents, and tears streamed down his cheeks. He says, however, that years later, at the memorial service for his father, "I had a relative lack of emotion, feeling more numb or just looking for the grief but not seeing it or finding it welling up within me.

"My sister erupted at one point, feeling like the other family members were not showing the appropriate amount of tears or grief. She was blubbering all over everywhere, and she was angry. She said, 'You all just didn't love Dad like I loved him. You didn't have the amount of love that I did.' Mom answered, 'Be very, very careful of what you assume about how other people grieve. What you just said about Mateen is not true. We just had a good conversation about your father and about our feelings, so don't you assume that because people aren't grieving the way you are that they're not dealing with the reality of your father's death.'"

While most of the men we interviewed reported that their wives had been very supportive, some expressed that their wives had difficulty in understanding what they were going through. One man replied, "My wife was most concerned over my lack of grieving. It reminded her of her dad and his dominance and control." Another explained that his wife had never gotten to know his father very well. He told us, "Through the process, she saw how much he meant to me." Another man said that his wife couldn't understand why he couldn't get over it and get on with life. "After all," she would remind him, "your dad is in heaven."

If a woman's grieving style is different from her husband's, she may misunderstand him. If a woman talks and cries, she may take personally her husband's withdrawal and introversion. Or if she processes things internally, her husband's tears may be disconcerting. Almost all wives will be upset if the husband expresses anger to her or the family. Very few will be able to identify with every issue that the husband is dealing with, such as identity or mortality.

For me the problems would cascade or rapidly switch back and forth. I'd picture my kids attending my deathbed; I'd see my father fishing; I'd regret things left unsaid; I'd fear my future responsibilities—all in a single minute. It was overwhelming, and it was difficult for my wife to cope with what was happening to me. (Bruce Barton)

Now What?

All this emotion, or lack of it, feelings of guilt and regret and rage, shocks and aftershocks, and potential for misunderstanding can be confusing. It's difficult for a son to know how to respond.

The first step is to allow plenty of time for the reality of your father's death to sink in and for you to process what has happened and its effects on you. Roll with the aftershocks; don't fight them. And don't do anything impetuous or drastic.

During this time, be patient with yourself. It is *your* process that you are going through, no one else's. It may be helpful to get away from the noise and bustle, to think and pray. Allow God to put the pieces back in *his* good time. Express *all* your feelings to God—he understands. Jeff B. says, "Go to a place and literally cry out your feelings to God. The hurt never goes away and can't be filled by other people—only by your heavenly Father." You may want to keep a journal of your thoughts and feelings. Some men find it helpful to write tributes or poems.

Next, rebuild slowly. Keep up your health, and find someone with whom you can talk, freely and honestly. If your wife seems to understand, start there, but also seek out a good male friend, preferably one who has also experienced father-loss. Roger advises, "Talk about it with other men whose fathers have recently died; process the experience."

Yes, you will continue to miss your father—you may never get back to "normal." But God can use this for your good; it can be a life-changing event.

"As Christians, I think we have life-changing, life-shaping experiences—when we become a Christian or when we dedicate our lives to the Lord. But I can say without a doubt that the death of my father is the most profound experience of my life, no question."

—DICK EPPS

WHAT DO YOU THINK?

1. When do you miss your father the most?

2. What aftershocks to his death did you experience?

3. What tends to trigger memories of your father and feelings about his death?

4. What emotions surprised you at the funeral? Since then?

5. How do you feel on Father's Day?

6. When have you felt anger or rage concerning your father's death?

7. How have you dealt with your anger?

8. What do you think it will take for you to "get over" your father's death?

9. In what ways has your faith helped you deal with your grief?

4

THE TALLEST TREE
Feeling Alone and Vulnerable

The tallest tree in the forest—that's how one man described how he pictured himself after his father's death. "The tallest tree"—alone, above, vulnerable to wind and lightning.

Jerry W. became the "tallest tree" at a very young age.

"The highest calling you could ever have would be as a minister and then win souls for Christ. That's what my dad thought," Jerry shares. And his father fulfilled that calling, focusing all his energies on spreading the Good News, traveling from pulpit to pulpit, broadcasting daily devotions on the radio, planting churches, starting an orphanage, serving on boards, and mentoring pastors and new believers.

Young Jerry idolized his father, but they spent little time together because of the demands of the ministry. Jerry says, "The only way I'd ever see my father, besides in the pulpit, was to try and stay awake at night until he got home, because he would always be gone in the morning. Sometimes I would climb in his bed to sleep, knowing that he would wake me up when he came home."

But the night before Jerry's eighth birthday, his father didn't make it home. Jerry explains, "It was Sunday morning, my birthday, and we were getting ready to go to church. I was already in the car in the garage, waiting there, with the garage door open. We just assumed that Dad was already at church. But a car stopped, and some ministers came up the front walk, and I had a feeling that something had happened to my dad. I got out and went into the house and saw my mother in the kitchen, just crushed."

Jerry soon learned that his father, who had been at a pastors conference, had heard of a woman in a hospital who had requested prayer, late at night. Jerry remembers, "Dad went and prayed for her right after midnight, and he was dead tired from all the meetings. He fell asleep at the wheel coming back and hit a bridge embankment on the turnpike."

> *"A part of you goes with your father. He could bring it out of you like no one else can."*
>
> —DR. KEN BOA

Jerry explains that the funeral was the biggest one that Tulsa had seen to that point, and it took three hours for all the ministers to share what his father had meant to them. Looking back, he marvels at all his father had accomplished by the age of 45.

Some of the ministers and others took Jerry aside, trying to console him. Unfortunately, in trying to make sense of the death, they said, "The Lord called him home," "His work on earth is finished," and "They need him more there." Jerry reflects, "All those strange messages, but nobody worked with me on what they meant. So I became angry with God for 'calling him home.' I felt cheated. Then, at night, I'd hear my mother crying and praying in the bedroom, 'O dear God, I can't go on! What will I do?'—just crying her heart out. I was the youngest of four. I'm sure that each sibling responded differently, but the way that impacted me was that I started becoming very responsible at a young age.

"I typed up a little card, 'Jerry's Lawn-mowing Service,' and I didn't even have a lawn mower. I asked Mom to get me one for Christmas—I would repay her. I was just eight and could hardly reach the handle and push the mower. But my business flourished. When I heard my mother wondering how she could go on, I decided that I wouldn't be a burden—I would help out financially."

Jerry also remembers that during the next few years, some men came alongside and became, in effect, father substitutes, taking him fishing and helping in other ways.

Now fast-forward several decades. Jerry is an adult, a college graduate, happily married, and a successful businessman. Jerry and his wife, Margaret, have no children of their own.

Every year, for a month or so, Jerry goes to Arkansas to retreat from the bustle of the office and suburban traffic. On one of those trips, after the worship service at a small country church, while talking with the pastor, Jerry learned about a boy named James. Jerry explains, "James is ten years old. His father died when he was eight. To supplement her income, James's mother has ten foster kids and two of her own in a doublewide trailer. I met James and got to know him and his situation. One day James said, 'Your father died when you were eight too?' Then he added, 'I'm trying to start a lawn-mowing service.'

"I said, 'How would you like to come work with me, over on my land? I've got some brush clearing to do.' He agreed, and I worked with him for a couple of days. He was asking me so many questions. I thought, *Here's a little kid who is ten years old. What a chance to give to him*. I watched him pick up the brush pile and push his mower. I saw him work hard to do a good job."

Jerry saw potential in the boy, and he saw himself. So he decided to spend more time with him. He remembers thinking, "I wish we were down here more, because this kid could be exceptional—he's a hard worker and he's thinking on his own." Jerry says, "He asked me about business. And I thought, *Man, that's exactly the way I would have been if somebody had come alongside me.* I asked him how he felt about his father. He began to really open up with me. I had heard that he was in counseling but that he would just sit there and wouldn't answer any questions. But out of that setting, with someone he could relate to, he opened up.

"I was blessed to have a wonderful father who was accessible to me from the earliest years of childhood. I'm told that when I was two years of age, my family lived in a one-bedroom apartment, and my little bed was located beside that of my parents. My father said later that it was very common during that time for him to awaken at night to a little voice that was whispering, 'Daddy? Daddy?' My father would answer quietly, 'What, Jimmy?' And I would say, 'Hold my hand!' Dad would reach across the darkness and grope for my little hand, finally just engulfing it in his own. He said the instant he had my hand firmly in his grip, my arm would become limp and my breathing deep and regular. I'd immediately gone back to sleep. You see, I only wanted to know that he was there!"

—DR. JAMES DOBSON. *BRINGING UP BOYS* (WHEATON, ILL.: TYNDALE HOUSE PUBLISHERS, 2001), 58–59.

"Later, I kept thinking how I could impact more people like that—he's just one kid. But then I thought, *It's not about the numbers.* Although James needs what I am doing for him, I learn much about myself by interacting with him." Jerry adds, "I believe that my limited experience with the boy has contributed to my continued healing. Our time together is as important to me as it is to him. And I think back to the times when I went fishing with the men in the church. Those were good times, but they could have been so much more. I could have been impacted by these men a lot more if they had not only taken me fishing but also had asked me about what I experienced around my father's death and had given me counsel."

As "the tallest tree," Jerry has survived, and thrived, and now he's helping another son do the same.

Though only eight, Jerry's response is typical for a son of any age who loses his father—feeling alone and isolated, trying to make sense of the situation and filled with questions.

WHAT NOW?

The plaintive cry of Jerry's mother reflects what many sons have felt, "What will I do? What now?" They feel lost and alone, as though life's foundation has been pulled away.

Bill W., a solid man in his forties, successful in business and active in his church and community, reports, "There I was, a grown man with a wife and three kids; yet I was wondering, can I make it now? Will it be OK? I felt a real loss of security."

Now an assistant director of world missions for a church denomination, Byron was 47 when his father died at 75 years of age. Although his dad had suffered for quite some time, and his death was a relief, Byron also felt suddenly insecure when his father died. He explains, "Just knowing Dad was always there to call when I needed him was a source of stability in my life. Suddenly that was gone forever."

Knowing that you're out there, alone, without your usual support, can feel strange, almost frightening.

WHY ME?

Another question commonly asked (though usually not aloud) is, "Why me?" We know that tragedies strike and that people die, but those terrible things happen to *other* families, *other* people, not us. We feel singled out and wonder why this had to come . . . to us. This response is normal in any painful experience but especially where death is concerned.

As young people, we assumed that pain was the exception, especially if we grew up in middle-class America. Over the years, as we matured, living through the aging process, we gained firsthand knowledge that pain and suffering are common occurrences—the rule and not the exception to life. We learned, in fact, that when something "good" happens, we should ask, "Why me?"

Yet, even though we know that truth, *this* event, this death, hits us hard, and we ask the question. And in asking it we assume that no else has experienced what we are going through, that we are the only ones. No one else knows; no one understands. In reality, sons have been experiencing this trauma and these emotions since Creation. The fact that this book has been written should be evidence enough. And that's why it helps to talk with other men who have lost their fathers—they really do "feel your pain."

Sons miss their dads desperately and don't want to stand there alone.

WHY DOESN'T THE WORLD STOP?

To many boys, Dad is bigger than life. He's the greatest and the best. When the father dies, these sons can't fathom how life can just go on in his community, neighborhood, work, and church. "Don't you realize what just happened?" they want to scream. "A *great* man died!" The son's life will never be the same, and he believes that's the way everyone else should feel.

I remember thinking over and over that the people at the church and in the community really didn't know Dad. They didn't know him as a young man and as a father, the way I had known him. I wanted them to realize what we all had lost. So I wrote my reflections about Dad, probably three pages—even mentioning his athletic and musical abilities—and had the minister read it at the funeral. (Dave Veerman)

Men we interviewed sent us tributes they had written, essays and poems honoring their fathers. Written with love, they wanted to honor Dad and to spread the word about the kind of man he was.

Paul L., a ministry executive in Atlanta, organized his tribute in the following categories: Dad's work on earth; Dad's service in the church; Dad's love for God; Dad's care and love for the family; Our gratitude to you on Dad's behalf.

It begins, "Many of you know that Dad was a hard worker, but he never seemed to complain about it. He worked in the pop factory and in a farm store, was a farmer, a custodian, a bus driver, and a truck driver. You name it; he probably hauled it. He owned his own trucking business and worked with my brother for a while, as well." This tribute highlights ordinary life—no extraordinary feats or accomplishments—but that's the point. Paul wanted everyone to know about his father, a good man, faithful and true, who would be missed. It's as though Paul is saying, "Dad may seem ordinary, but he was much more—he was special and he meant so much to me!"

Many of the sons we interviewed who were young when their fathers died reported that they were impressed by how many people attended the funeral. Until then they hadn't realized how many lives their fathers had touched.

Bill K. remembers, "So many people shared how Dad had helped them. So many people came. I was surprised that he had known and had helped so many." Bill's brother Dave also remembers being impressed with how many people were at the funeral. He says, "It was a long funeral procession, especially for someone who had been so lonely. Hundreds came."

But then, shortly thereafter, many of these men wondered where everyone had gone. They felt the contrast and the resulting loneliness. Usually people expect everyone to return to normal a few weeks after the funeral. The father's death will still be central in the son's mind, however, while everyone else has moved on. People who haven't had the same experience may not have perspective or empathy.

"I watched a man die last night. Hospice Room 436 lay unusually quiet—except for labored breathing, a sound like a man running a long final lap. His blue hospital gown rose and fell on the heaving chest.

"The black magic marker tag above the bed read: 'Gillis, Algerd.' Al was the father of Michael, my friend. When my dad died eight years ago, Michael stood by me. When the sympathy cards had stopped coming and I began the terrifying freefall into grief, Michael had been my parachute. Now I could stand with him in vigil at his father's deathbed."

—KEVIN A. MILLER. "THE NIGHT I LEARNED WHAT REALLY MATTERS." CUSTOMZINES eARTICLE (AUGUST 6, 2002).

AM I AN ORPHAN?

Another "tallest tree" experience is feeling like an orphan. The other trees have fallen away, leaving you standing alone. When a parent dies, that thought intrudes. Children of all ages feel this way after both parents are gone. But men seem to have these feelings when their father dies, even if he is the first parent to go.

Oliver says, "The interesting thing about losing my father and now again with my mother is the awareness of my abandoned-ness

"Many adults experience a deep and complicated grief, according to experts. Compounding the sorrow over the loss of a parent are feelings of abandonment, a loss of a connection to the past, and the recognition of one's own mortality.

"'When my father died after a long illness in 1990, one of my first thoughts was when my mother dies, I'm going to be an orphan,' said Kyle Nash (a thanatologist working at the University of Chicago Hospital's McLean Center for Clinical and Medical Ethics). 'Chronologically, we may be however old, but deep, deep, deep in our core we are still the children we once were, and at times of vulnerability, we revert back to that . . .'

"'When they die, you're nobody's child,' said family therapist Audrey K. Gordon, preceptor for end-of-life care at the University of Illinois at Chicago Medical School. A hospice founder, assistant to Elisabeth Kubler-Ross and former professor at UIC, Gordon was a pioneer in the death and dying movement . . .

"'When September 11 happened, the first thing I wanted to do was call my father and get reassurance that it's going to be OK,' said Kate Marrin, a mediator with the Cook County Circuit Court's office of marriage and family counseling. 'You lose that too—that reassurance that things are going to be OK.'"

—MEGHAN MUTCHLER DEERIN. "NOBODY'S CHILD: ADULTHOOD DOESN'T ELIMINATE THE PAIN OF BECOMING AN ORPHAN." *CHICAGO TRIBUNE* (CHICAGO, ILL.: JUNE 2, 2002).

---

and my orphaned-ness, being an orphan—and how that can attack in the times I least expect it. It's almost like an ambush. I'm going along loving God and thankful for my salvation; then I turn on the television and happen to notice something or other, a word someone has said, an image or something like that, and all of a sudden my mind is full of my father and my loss."

THAT'S ME!

What makes the "tallest tree" experience so poignant is the fact that a son finds out who he is as a man from his father.

In his best-selling book *Wild at Heart*, counselor and lecturer John Eldredge writes, "Masculinity is *bestowed*. A boy learns who he is and what he's got from a man, or the company of men. He cannot learn it any other place. He cannot learn it from other boys, and he cannot learn it from the world of women. The plan from the beginning of time was that his father would lay the foundation for a young boy's heart, and pass on to him that essential knowledge and confidence in his strength. Dad would be the first man in his life, and forever the most important man. Above all, he would answer *the question* [Do I have what it takes? Am I a man?] for his son and give him his name. Throughout the history of man given to us in Scripture, it is the father who gives the blessing and thereby 'names' the son."[1]

Jeff B. reflects this truth when he says, "I am just like my dad. I see that as very positive because we had a good relationship. We had our moments of disagreements, but I very much looked up to my father. As I get older, I find myself becoming even more like Dad, and I'd love to tell him that and to get his counsel."

I felt very alone the first three years after my father died—with my friends, in my family, at work, and at church. I was alone, even in a crowd. I know now that I was turning inward to find a way to think about all that had happened and how life had changed. But I had also taken a huge blow to my identity as a son. When I was a teenager, I had a rough time identifying with my father. We didn't seem to connect on many points. He was in business; I went into ministry. His

first love was fishing; I wasn't that interested. As I got older, how-
ever, I began to identify with him more and find common ground. It
was just getting good when he died.

From my high school memories, I particularly remember my dad at
the dinner table. He would always seem to have a crick in his neck,
caused by the stress of his work. So he would rub that knot of muscle.
Today, I deal with the same kind of crick in the neck. When I am tense
and irritable from the pressures of my business, I understand him
more. This helps me act differently toward my kids. (Bruce Barton)

NOT LIKE DAD

Men who have *not* enjoyed a positive, affirming relationship
with their fathers will often work hard to be different. For
example, Bill J. reflects, "My dad never sought counsel on anything. I determined not to be like that."

These men determine to break the cycle of negative role
modeling, alcoholism, and even abuse.

- Tom T. says, "Dad and I would have about five
  minutes of conversation, and that would be it. I don't
  think we had the bond that some fathers and sons
  have. It made me committed to spending as much time
  with my children as possible and bonding and telling
  them how I feel. I also don't let a day go by without
  telling my kids that I love them, being verbal about it,
  and not just verbal but physical—hugs. I am very
  sensitive to the fact that they need to be told and
  shown that I care about them."

- Chuck, a ministry executive from the Twin Cities,
  explains, "Knowing the way our parents were,
  especially my father, my wife and I got on our knees.
  We knew we had to break the chain. But now it's

coming out again—the dominance issue—where I have to be in control, just like my father. It's a constant breaking of the chain."

- Dave says, "Because of my father's bad example, I'm a better father. I don't remember my father doing anything with us, but I'm there for my kids. In fact, I probably overcompensate. My daughter, now a freshman in college, recently wrote, 'I've never thanked you for always being there, always being positive.'"

These men determined to be different. Each one would say that he had realized the problem and had made this decision years earlier, but his father's death had brought the issue forcefully to the forefront of his mind and will. Suddenly, he knew that he never would be able to change things about his father or find reconciliation with him. Now it was totally up to him, the surviving son, to change, to alter the family pattern, to be different.

No Dad at All

A father's death can even affect a son with whom he has had virtually no contact. Again, this is an issue of identity or self-worth.

Rob, an investment counselor from North Carolina, was raised in a children's home. His father had tried to commit suicide when Rob was just a baby. The gunshot attempt had rendered Rob's father mentally incompetent and confined to a distant nursing home. Rob's mother, struggling with her own mental and emotional issues and unable to care for a small son, placed Rob in the orphanage. Rob never knew his father, yet, as a young adult in his late twenties, he went to Georgia for the graveside service after his father died. Rob wondered, "Am I doomed to be crazy like my parents?" Rob had forgiven his father many years before, but he was surprised by his feelings as he stood at the graveside: *You were such a wimp,* he thought. *How can I be the son of such a wimp? I am not going to be like you!*

Identity issues like these will heighten the feelings of loss and abandonment.

"I wanted so much to be able to just capture moments. I would have been happy for just a few moments of affirmation or encouragement or connection. When that doesn't happen, it leaves a real hole in a person's heart."

—DR. JOHN TRENT

ON MY OWN

The overwhelming feeling at this point is vulnerability. With the father gone, the son can feel exposed, abandoned, on his own, at risk. These feelings come first at the funeral and then return, as we have heard men testify, during moments of crisis and responsibility. The car breaks; the marriage flounders; the boss rants; the stock market plummets. We may be used to calling Dad for advice about work, family issues, church, or just life. Or we may have turned to him for help in remodeling the house or in other projects and challenges, depending on his area of expertise. And even if we never asked Dad for a loan, we knew he was there to bail us out, if we needed it. Then he's gone and we're alone and on our own.

The father often functions as the shield, the safety net, and the solid foundation, even when we don't recognize those roles. With Dad around, we feel more secure and safe. Without him we can feel vulnerable and afraid. We may even wonder, "What do I do now? Where can I go for help? Who will protect me?"

The tree may be tall and strong, but it's also up there and out there.

You may feel like the tallest tree, just waiting for lightning to strike. But look around. Many others are standing with you.

WHAT DO YOU THINK?

1. Where do you stand in the sibling order (for example, oldest, middle child, baby of the family)?

2. How do you think your place in the family affected your reactions to your father's death?

3. If you have a sister, how did her response compare to yours?

4. How can people feel alone when surrounded by others?

5. In what ways was your identity redefined after your father died?

6. When did you feel as though you were "the tallest tree"? How did you respond?

7. How did your father shape or thwart your identity development?

8. At what times do you feel most vulnerable? Instead of your father, where can you now turn for help?

5

MORTALITY EXPOSED
Realizing That Life Is Short

We deny it. We don't want to think about it. We act as though we will escape it. But despite all denials and avoidance techniques, eventually we must stare the truth concerning our mortality straight in the eye: one of these days, we will die, each and every one of us.

Let's face it. No one wants to talk about death, especially one's own. It's too unnerving, unsettling, premature. And, especially when we're young (let's say under 40), when we *do* think about it, we assume that death will come many years from now, way in the future. Need proof? Consider our lifestyles, past and present. We live as though we are invincible. As daring teenagers and young adults, we used to thrive on risky behaviors, making destructive lifestyle choices and acquiring bad habits. We still drive as though we're immortal (despite statistics, traffic accidents, and public service announcements). It's a myth, of course. But we buy it . . . until the truth shakes us awake.

REALITY CHECK

That's what it's like when a father dies. Suddenly a surviving son is confronted with the truth that life is terminal, and death is real, and that he, too, will someday die. That realization can hit at almost any funeral, but most powerfully and relentlessly at our father's. It hits especially hard at that moment because, as we have discussed, we see ourselves in our father's place. "When he died, so, in a way, did I," said one man.

Mark N., a well-known and respected professor and historian, was 46 when his father, a mechanical engineer, died at 74. The funeral was private and in the evening. Mark says, "I remember the shock of my father's death. For a while I didn't sleep very well. What hit me the most was the mortality that everyone possesses."

Oliver recalls his experience this way: "The reality of one's mortality is something that you can actually feel and taste. It's like someone coming up from behind, and you sense the person. The person may be walking at a distance right now and hasn't quite caught up to you but really is there. So you begin to realize that death is inevitable, that it's getting closer. Sometimes that gets you angry, but you don't know why."

Spike, a Chicago radio personality, uses the same picture in describing his feelings: "My father's death and the funeral made me understand that death is part of life. It sneaks up on you. I knew this already, of course, but I was hit with the thought that we're all going to die. So in a way, my father's death was sort of a rite of passage—I survived it. I had days where I felt down after that, but it didn't wipe me out."

Oliver explains how this powerful sense of his mortality affected him. He says, "I love life. I love living. I want to live for as long as I possibly can. But with the experience of the loss of my father, it suddenly dawned on me—69—that's not very old. Then I remembered that my father's father had died at about 50 or 51 years old. And I started to check it out and discovered that no man in my family had lived to 70. That's a sobering thought, particularly when you're pushing 50."

Jim G. recalls thinking about being ready for death. "Am I

ready to die? In one way, yes. I'm sure when I die I'll go to heaven, and that will be fine. But what will happen to my kids? So when would I be *really* ready to die?"

When your father dies, death becomes real, and personal.

IT'S OVER

Another reality we have to face is that *this* man is gone. It's over, final, and nothing more can be written to his story.

On this point, Oliver shares, "In our tradition, the casket was opened again, at the funeral in the church. When I looked at him there, it was quite obvious that he was dead. That struck me, the finality, because already I could see the deterioration of the body. Although he hadn't been in the greatest of health, he had been working, alive, and making a whole lot of noise at the body shop he owned. Then I realized that in front of me is a corpse; yet this corpse is my father. These are conflicting emotions. I was drawn to my father, but I was repelled by the fact that it was a corpse. The deadness of death is very stinging. I remember that about the funeral."

Dick H., a career-path consultant from Massachusetts, was in his early thirties when his father died. His father was a construction worker (and drove a grader for many years), a town construction supervisor, and a dairy farmer. Dick describes his father as a hard worker, positive, and faithful to the family and to church.

Dick can't remember much about the funeral service, but he recalls sitting in the car behind the hearse, just before the long, winding drive to the cemetery. He says, "It sort of struck me when they brought the casket into the hearse and then shut the door. Boom—that was my dad, I thought. There was a finality to it."

He explains that he was surprised by "just death itself, because I had never experienced it that close. And it was so unexpected because he had just been given a medical A+. So, at the hospital,

"The last thing my youngest son said to me before I raced out the door to go to O'Hare was, 'When will you be home, Dad?'

"That's the way most kids are when their parents leave. They don't really care where mom or dad is going, what they're going to do when they get there, or who they're going to see. They want to know when you'll be back.

"I told him that I would be back in a couple of days. He said, without looking up from his cereal bowl, 'OK . . . bye . . . love you.' And I was out the door.

"That same scene plays out every day, everywhere, and nobody thinks much about it. Until the plane crash. Or the hotel fire. Or the drunken driver. Or the heart attack . . .

"The next time I leave home, one of my children is certain to ask, 'Dad, when will you be back?'

"And even though I know it's not a sure thing, I'll give them the same, straight answer as always. In an hour. In time for your game. Before you go to bed.

"The truth is, it doesn't really matter when you'll be home. What counts is what you did before you left."

—CHUCK GOUDIE. "THERE'S NO SURE ANSWER TO 'WHEN WILL YOU BE HOME, DAD?'" *DAILY HERALD* (NAPERVILLE, ILL.: UNIVERSAL PRESS SYNDICATE, AUG 27, 2001), 9.

---

even though the doctor told me that my father's condition was very, very serious, I knew in my heart he wouldn't die. So what caught me by surprise was death itself—that a man who was so healthy could die."

Mateen says, "When you see the effect of death face-to-face, taking someone you love away from you, the finality of that makes you wish you had taken the passing of time more seriously. You have no more opportunities to build that relationship or to rebuild bridges."

"I thought, *Now it's over—he can't do anything to hold me back*," reflects Jerry H. "But I'll never have the opportunity to right things again!"

And John D. adds, "The irreversibility is what hit me."

This truth is a bitter pill to swallow.

"My father's death has a thousand endings. I continue to absorb its messages and meanings. He stripped death of its spooky morbidity and made it tangible and passionate. He prepared me in some way for my own death. He showed me the responsibility of the living to the dying. But the most enduring thought was expressed by my sister. Afterward, she told me she had learned something from all this. I asked her what it was. She said, 'Nobody should have to die alone.'"

—STEVE MARTIN. "THE DEATH OF MY FATHER." *THE NEW YORKER* (NEW YORK, N.Y.: JUNE 17 & 24, 2002), 87.

OUT OF OUR CONTROL

Compounding the problem is the illusion of control. We actually believe we can control what happens to us, especially when we are young and have not experienced much of life. So we talk about choices and the future as though we can predict it for certain. And, as men, we are used to fixing what's broken, taking charge, and making sure that what's supposed to happen, happens. We organize, manage, and give orders. But ultimate control is a myth, an illusion. In the grand scheme of things, in matters of life and death and destiny, we are *not* in control.

We learn the truth when suddenly it happens, something unexpected and extraordinary, and we're knocked for a loop and back into reality. Ask anyone who has received *the call* . . . from the hospital or police station or relative. Or just remember where you were and how you felt on September 11, 2001, as you heard and saw the terrible events unfold in New York, Washington, D.C., and Pennsylvania.

A father's death is that kind of event, shaking our safe and predictable world. That wasn't supposed to happen to us, to our family . . . to me. It wasn't in the plan.

According to Elizabeth Levang, "Grief is the great emasculator. Most of us will know no other time in our lives when we have been so absolutely and completely stripped of control. This insecurity is especially intense for men whose identity, worth, and self-esteem are tied closely to issues of power and authority."[1]

She also writes, "Through personal tragedy we learn a disturbing and painful lesson: though life is often predictable, sometimes it is extremely unpredictable . . . When life doesn't go their way, men tend to feel powerless and angry . . . They sense rejection and brood about what has been lost . . . Filled with self-doubt, some men rely on sarcasm to lessen their disappointment. Their caustic attitude reflects disillusionment with life and the bitter feelings they hold inside."[2]

John D. found control, or the illusion of it, difficult to relinquish. He says, "That's because I consider myself to be a self-made person. My father's death changed my relationship with God. It was strained at first. You see, it's easy to talk about accepting God's will for your life, but it's harder to do it. I had just been 'talking the talk.' I learned that he's in charge, not me."

"I never dreamed it would be this way," Gordon admits. "I had it all figured out, or so I thought. But Dad's heart attack changed everything. I was pretty upset."

Tragedies burst the control bubble and infuriate us.

"Psychologist Roger Gould once said that midlife can 'slam us in the face like a steel door.' Up until his early thirties, a man tends to see the world as virtually limitless. And then, sometimes suddenly, sometimes gradually, loss moves from being a virtual stranger to a regular guest. A man's friends and colleagues start dying. His children move away. His sex drive slackens. His career opportunities dwindle. Add to this the death of a parent, and the future of the midlife man can seem depressing and frightening."

—NEIL CHETHIK. FATHERLOSS (NEW YORK: HYPERION, 2001), 87.

A MORNING FOG

In addition to facing the truth about death, at this time we also face the truth about life. Suddenly we realize just how short it is, how quickly time passes. And we mutter, "Where did the years go?" "It seems like just yesterday," and other telling phrases.

The idea of a "long life" touches on yet another misconception of youth—the length of a year or a decade or a life. For a child, a year seems very long; for an adult, it seems like an instant. That's because as a person ages, a year represents an increasingly smaller portion of that person's life. If a junior-high history teacher says, "That happened *only* ten years ago," the students think, Only *ten years? That's more than two thirds of my lifetime!* But adults, especially those older than fifty, feel as though the events of a decade ago occurred just yesterday. Time passes ever more quickly as we age. Life is short.

And do you recall, as a child, projecting yourself into the future? You may have thought something like this: *Let's see, in 1990, I'll be ___ years old, and in 2000, I'll be _____.* Most young children have trouble imagining themselves older than 25 or 30. And 40 seems ancient.

Well, you're there now. It didn't take very long, did it?

Or remember reading the obituary of a stranger, someone in his or her seventies or eighties? You may have thought, "It's not so bad, because he was old," or, "She had a good life." The death of someone "elderly" didn't seem nearly so tragic as if the deceased had been a younger man or woman.

But when someone *you love* dies—no matter how old he or she may be—death came too soon, life went by too fast. And for many, the person died too young.

So a father's death brings another reality bite: *Life is short no matter how long you live . . . and mine will be over before I know it.* No wonder James wrote, "How do you know what will happen tomorrow? For your life is like the morning fog—it's here a little while, then it's gone. What you ought to say is, 'If the Lord wants us to, we will live and do this or that.' Otherwise you will be boasting about your own plans, and all such boasting is evil" (4:14–16).

Hit with the finality and inevitability of death, the lack of control, and the brevity of life, our mourning takes a turn. As we grieve our father-loss, sorrowing over his death, we also grieve for what we are learning about ourselves and about life.

When the reality hits that we, too, will someday be laid to rest, we can be tempted to turn inward with dread. This life path leads to depression and despair. The specter of death drains the life from today's joys and opportunities.

On the other hand, this heightened awareness of our own mortality can be a milepost in our lives, a stepping-stone to greater maturity. We can look death in the eye and move on in the right direction.

First, this new understanding of our finiteness can move us toward God. As Roger explains, "I suddenly realized my mortality. That's where my faith really made a difference. Now I'm asking God to help me go deeper in relationship with my children and their spouses."

Jim F., a financial consultant from Illinois, also expresses this move toward God. "My father's sudden death helped me realize the need to truly have God at the center of my life, inasmuch as life is so fragile and really so short. It pointed me to a deeper dependence on our heavenly Father." He continues, "It put me in touch with my own mortality and more closely with two additional truths: (1) I would at some point meet the Savior face to face; (2) I would be reunited with my earthly father too."

Paul V. reflects, "Dad's death confirmed the fact that life is terminal, life goes on, and life with Christ is better and more rewarding than life without him."

Second, realizing that time is short can motivate us to see life as a precious gift and to value every moment. David expresses this powerfully in Psalm 39: "'LORD, remind me how brief my time on earth will be. Remind me that my days are numbered, and that my life is fleeing away. My life is no longer than the width of my hand. An entire lifetime is just a moment to you; human existence is but a breath' . . . And so, Lord, where do I put my hope? My only hope is in you" (vs. 4–5, 7).

The challenge for Christian men is not to respond on the hedonistic level, thinking, for example, "Since life is short, I'll buy a sports car, go on more vacations, get a new woman in my life . . ." Instead, we should determine to live as better stewards of our remaining twenty, thirty, or forty years and to go deeper spiritually and relationally. We need to focus on the right that we are doing and also find contentment in God and in the friends and family he has put in our lives.

In this regard, Jim W. says, "My father's death helped me sort out my priorities. I was amazed at how quickly a life could be distilled into a few sentences. And I wondered what my obituary would say."

"My father may be the only person in the history of the world who changed himself because he despised a character in literature who struck chords of horror in himself that he could not face. He had the best second act in the history of fathering. He was the worst father I have ever heard of, and I will go to my own grave believing that. But this most immovable of men found it within himself to change. I could not believe how much I had come to love my father when he died on May 11, 1998 . . .

"He died a richly beloved man, even an adored one. His children were bereft at his funeral and remain so to this day."

—PAT CONROY. MY LOSING SEASON (NEW YORK: DOUBLEDAY, 2002). EXCERPTED IN AARP MODERN MATURITY (NOV/DEC 2002), 80.

Ray H., a securities broker, was 26 when his dad died at the age of 59 of stomach cancer. Although Ray did not have a good relationship with his father, his dad's death was a pivotal point in Ray's life. He explains, "I was a driven sort of guy to begin with, but when I realized how young my dad had died, I knew that I had no time to waste if I was going to make something of my life before it ended."

Jeff B. adds, "Undoubtedly my father's death helped me understand that we all die and that life is short, so I'm going to pour every day into my boys. In some ways, I didn't get that from Dad because of his sickness. I need to give my sons as much of myself while I can."

THE NEXT IN LINE

Coming to grips with our own mortality hits us where we live—it's intensely personal. At the same time, however, we realize that our whole generation is now exposed, especially if we are adults and family men when our fathers die. It becomes painfully obvious that we and our peers are the new old folks—we're the next in line.

Mark S. explains, "My father's death and its impact has made me realize that I am the 'frontline' in the senior generation. I had a much greater sense of my mortality."

Oliver says it this way, "You recognize, especially if you've had any kind of relationship with your father, that this is it. This is the end of one line of people that really can never be repeated again. You become the next in line. People who haven't gone through this experience don't quite understand."

If you have ever attended a high-school reunion, you know that you can't fool any of your former classmates about your age. No matter how successful you have been at retaining your youthful glow—exercise, special diet, make-up, cosmetic surgery, new wardrobe—everyone knows how old you are. So you may look better than the other fifty-year-olds in the room, but the fact remains—you are fifty too.

You also share life experiences—education, marriage, children—and the frustrating evidences of aging, including weight distribution, receding hairlines, and physical challenges. You are traveling through life together. It feels a bit strange, actually, to be grouped for that weekend by age.

An adult son feels similarly when his father dies, even if his father is the first known person of that age group to pass away. Up till then, the older generation has served as sort of a buffer. The man is known as so-and-so's son, and his children have their grandpa. Suddenly, however, the mantle is passed, and the son stands at the forefront of the family, leading the charge into the future. He can't fool anyone, particularly himself, anymore. These feelings are not limited to the eldest son; it's a generational thing.

IN HIS PLACE

The prospect of taking Dad's place can be intimidating and daunting. Dr. Ken Canfield (The National Center for Fathering) reports that in a study of 2,066 fathers, "father satisfaction" (the satisfaction in being a father) dipped significantly after the father's death. He says, "There's the sense of exposure— I'm the head of the clan."

Neil Chethik writes, "A father's death creates a hole in a man's life. He is suddenly alone in a profound way. He must take more responsibility for himself and, often, his extended family. And he must begin to face his own mortality. For the first time, there is no giant of a man standing between him and the doors of death."[3]

Again, this realization can be depressing or exhilarating, stifling or motivating. It's our choice.

A month after my father's death, I received a very encouraging letter from my father-in-law. I appreciated the letter when I received it, and a month later, I really needed it. He wrote: "My father had a very uncomfortable last few years, and it hurt to see someone who was so dynamic and virile go downhill so fast. I know how you must have felt. Unfortunately these things happen to almost everyone, and it is a part of maturing . . . Love, Dad." I appreciated getting the letter. My father-in-law was indicating his understanding of what I was *going through. This was my first inkling that something positive would come from it. I would grow from the experience.* (Bruce Barton)

Dick E. felt the full weight of this new responsibility. He says, "I realized that now no father stood between me and *the* Father. He's gone. It's up to me."

This change in status caused Ralph to reevaluate his lifestyle. He explains, "I realized that I was the older generation, more responsible to really be a good dad, a better dad, to take time for my kids."

> *"Remember your Creator in the days of your youth, before the days of trouble come and the years approach when you will say, 'I find no pleasure in them.'"*
>
> —ECCLESIASTES 12:1 (NIV)

Psalm 90:12 declares, "Teach us to make the most of our time, so that we may grow in wisdom."

Ironically, Dick E. was speaking at a youth retreat when he received word that his father had been killed. Dick's text that evening was Ecclesiastes, and he was talking about Solomon's search for purpose in life. He says, "This was so meaningful for me because I had to face that question personally, right then. I suddenly realized that eternity was just around the corner. Dad was just sitting there in his car when boom! he was gone. It was a profound philosophical/spiritual experience. I saw the uncertainty of life, and I realized that I needed to do what really mattered in my remaining days, what would count for eternity."

WHAT DO YOU THINK?

1. What about the funeral symbolized finality for you?
2. When did you become painfully aware of your own mortality? How did it make you feel?

3. When are you most tempted to think and live as though you are in total control of what happens to you? Why can this be a problem?

4. How did you experience the feeling of powerlessness or loss of control?

5. At what times are you most aware of the brevity of life?

6. What can you do to "number your days"?

7. What steps can you take to add quality to your life?

8. By what hedonistic responses are you most tempted? Why those?

9. How has your father's death moved you closer to God?

10. What lifestyle changes have you made as a result of becoming aware of your mortality and the brevity of life? What changes should you make?

6

LOSS OF AUDIENCE
Missing the One Who Cheered Us On

"OK, you guys—from the right side, circle layups. Dribble all the way, get your own rebound, and then dribble to the basket at the other end. Four-dribble intervals between players. Start and end at the whistle." Coach Lundquist barked out his instructions as twelve nearly exhausted but still eager sophomore boys encircled him at the free-throw line. Then, after dividing the team into two groups, with six players at each basket, he blew the whistle and we began running again—dribbling and shooting, sweating and panting.

Minutes later, at a brief break and through sweat-filled eyes, I saw the man, standing at the far end of the gym, by the door at the edge of the bleachers. A big guy, six foot three and about 230 pounds, he would find it difficult to hide, but he wasn't trying to. He just wanted to observe without being too obvious and distracting the players. He had left work early to see his boy, this boy, practice basketball. With tie loosened and his overcoat draped over one arm, this lone spectator, my father, watched our routine of layups, drills, plays, and free throws.

That moment remains etched in my mind, a memory of Dad's love and interest in how I was doing. Later, he would comment on the team and on my play, and he would end with his trademark encouragement, *"Keep hustlin'!"*

In my mind's eye, I also see him at the JV football game, standing on the sidelines in the rain with a handful of other parents. We played, not on Friday nights in the stadium under the lights in front of the cheering home crowd, but on Wednesday afternoons or Saturday mornings on the practice field behind the high school and before our loyal family members. Who in their right mind would endure muddy shoes, cold hands, and wet clothes to watch adolescent boys in bulky equipment try to run, block, pass, catch, and tackle? My father. So, when my father died, I felt I had lost my audience, my cheering section. (Dave Veerman)

Many men who enjoyed a positive relationship with their fathers can identify with that experience. Sports and Dad—the

---

The fourth poem of "Memorial Quartet"

Will I ever hear a ball bounce on
a hardwood floor and not look up to seek
his face (and half expect to hear him give
the ref what for); or beat a frozen dawn
awake and silently steal down the stairs
and not in shadows think to catch a peek
of back bent over books as he prepares
for next week's class at Sunday school; or live
to see a child in church claw at his itching
tie and not remember our old strife;
or ever, to the last time I commit
a message to a child of mine, forget
the words—"I love you very much"—with which
he signed his letters, and defined his life?

—DR. MARK A. NOLL. SEASONS OF GRACE (GRAND
RAPIDS, MICH.: BAKER BOOK HOUSE, 1997), 64.

---

two go together. Dad watches, cheers, encourages, and coaches, and he loves every minute of it. The experience is not limited to sports. Sons with a wide variety of interests and abilities find their fathers closely observing their progress and attending every event possible.

The father of Mike S. was a tough-as-nails football and swimming coach for many years at a Chicago public high school. Mike, his older brother, and his sister were outstanding athletes in high school and college (and beyond). Their dad sacrificed to make every football game, wrestling meet, swim meet, baseball game, track meet, and speed-skating race he could. Mike says, "Dad would tell us, 'You only lose when you quit,' and that has become my way of thinking and living too. And he always signed his letters, 'Stay tough'—I sign the same way."

Mike followed his father into coaching and today serves as the head football coach at a college in the Midwest. Mike's most prized memento of his father is a picture of him standing on the sidelines during a hard-fought football game. His fist is in the air and his mouth is open, yelling instructions and encouragement to his team. The photograph hangs in Mike's office, and to him it embodies the essence of his father—tough and dedicated, coaching, encouraging, and cheering. Of his own children, Mike says, "I'm determined to pass on the legacy. I want my kids to know that I am who I am because of him. He had a great impact on me, and it makes me take seriously my job as a father."

Others describe a similar experience. Dick H. remembers, "Dad would go to every one of my basketball games, even though I rode the bench. He had to get up early the next morning and go to work. That's pretty doggone good, you know it?"

Losing that kind of support is huge. Phil V. shares, "Dad was my biggest fan. I lost my cheerleader and coach."

In addition, no one else cares as much about our children and their accomplishments as our parents. Others listen to our stories and show genuine interest—siblings, friends, coworkers, and neighbors—but not like Mom and Dad. That's how it should be, of course. The others have concerns of their own—marriages, careers, children, struggles, and successes, making it difficult for them to eagerly listen to us. But our parents want to hear it all. We are a vital part of their lives.

Dad can be a son's biggest fan, listening and offering advice and encouragement. So when Dad is gone, when he dies, there isn't just one less face in the crowd. It seems as though the whole crowd has disappeared.

This huge loss catches men by surprise. Many say that they fully expected to grieve but had no idea that they would miss their dads in this way.

Men miss being able to talk and share in four major areas: personal achievements, kids' news, parenting passages, and counsel.

PERSONAL ACHIEVEMENTS

No one appreciates a braggart. Boasting of personal accomplishments is impolite and highly self-centered. But reporting one's achievements is permitted and accepted between a parent and a child. "How did school go today?" asks Dad. "I got an A on my English paper," answers little Billy proudly, with a wide smile. "That's terrific," replies his father. "You are really doing well in school this year!"

Imagine a similar conversation between a child and a friend. The dialogue would vary considerably. We can enthusiastically announce good fortune and accomplishments to our parents, and they will listen, congratulate us, and then proudly repeat the news to others. All through our lives, through childhood and adolescence and into adulthood, they celebrate with us. So now, as adults, when we receive an award or promotion at work, we call home. When our kids achieve, we let Grandpa and

Grandma know. When we reach a personal milestone, Dad is often the first person we tell. He rejoices in each success.

Harry says, "When I'm at my kids' games, I think of my father and wish he could have seen them play. I also miss him when I'm at work because Dad never understood what I did for a career."

"I don't feel my dad's presence. But even all these years later, I feel his absence, and the fact that his presence isn't there. After my brother died, I was an only child. And Dad and Mom were always there for everything I was ever involved in. I didn't have to wonder if my mom or dad would be there. They always, always, always were."

—RON HUTCHCRAFT

Jeff R. became motivated by his dad's support. He says, "Dad's death spurred me on to want to be a good father to my kids. Dad was my number-one fan, so I wanted to be that for my kids in every area."

A father's approval can also motivate a boy and then a man to keep at a task and to do the best he can. Kevin explains, "During my high school and college years, Dad provided my main motivation for playing football. I knew that he loved to watch me play and succeed, so I continued, year after year, even though several times I felt like quitting. Mom affirmed, encouraged, and consoled me in every endeavor, but Dad pushed me to work hard, to excel, and to win."

Men keep this desire to please their fathers well into their adult years—as a worker, husband, father, church member, and other roles. This search for Dad's approval and affirmation is positive and good when it flows from a healthy father-son relationship. A son wants his father to be proud of him, so he revels in telling Dad about his achievements and awards. Months and even years after the father's death, a son can think, *I ought to tell Dad about this*, or, *Dad would love this!* Then he remembers, sadly, that his father is gone. He isn't around to answer the phone, meet for lunch, or read the letter. The audience has left.

This whole area of activities and performance can have a negative side as well. Unfortunately, some fathers push their sons to succeed in order to meet their own needs through their sons, often with tragic results. Others stand at a distance, seemingly uncaring and aloof. In both cases, the sons usually feel as though they have to earn their fathers' love and acceptance. They may double their efforts in an attempt to win approval. The father's death brings no relief. In fact, they often have an even more difficult time dealing with the loss because now they know that they will never have the chance to please their fathers, they'll never prove that they are good enough. The opportunity died along with Dad.

Ray K. knows that feeling. His father never got to see the fine husband and father that he has become. Ray remembers that after the birth of his first child, "All of a sudden I began to weep as I said 'father' and 'Erik,' realizing that Dad would never see my son."

"Each of us men is a little boy on the inside," explains Jim G. "Your dad's like a god to you. You want your dad to approve of you. You want to make your dad proud. I don't think you ever get rid of wanting to make your dad proud. So it makes perfect sense when you say if you feel that approval, the death is easier. If you didn't have that approval or didn't feel it, now you have the rest of your life with that vacuum. Who is going to fill in for your dad and say you're OK?"

"I walked into the bedroom where he lay, his mind alert but his body failing. He said, almost buoyantly, 'I'm ready now.' I understood that his intensifying rage of the last few years had been against death, and now his resistance was abating. I stood at the end of the bed, and we looked into each other's eyes for a long, unbroken time. At last he said, 'You did everything I wanted to do.'

"I said, 'I did it because of you.' It was the truth. Looking back, I'm sure that we both had different interpretations of what I meant."

—STEVE MARTIN. "THE DEATH OF MY FATHER." *THE NEW YORKER* (NEW YORK: JUNE 17 & 24, 2002), 87.

With Dad gone, we lose a deep well of affirmation and approval.

KIDS' NEWS

A popular bumper sticker reads, "Ask me about my grandchildren," proclaiming loudly the source of a grandparent's pride and joy. Check out your family's videos and look for the reactions of the grandparents at the birthday parties for your kids when they were very young. If you have not yet reached that stage of life, imagine how you will react at the happy occasions of your grandson or granddaughter. Certainly you will try to attend every special event in his or her life. And when you can't be there, you will want to hear a play-by-play description.

Mothers and fathers enjoy telling their parents all about the

Father's Day

"*Coach Darryl Sutter . . . made it known the other day that he was contemplating retiring to spend more time with his children. 'They can get along without me just fine,' Sutter said of the Blackhawks. 'But I have three little kids and one of them needs a lot of help . . .'*

"*Unlike other sports figures who've made similar statements, you tend to believe Sutter's sincerity. Sutter said he'll do what's 'best for my kids. I didn't come from a material world where you needed a million dollars or you were judged on how much money you made.'*

"*Good for him. You can see he cares. As we come up on Father's Day, it's really too bad that more people don't feel the same way . . .*

"*While I have a great deal to be thankful for, the keenest disappointment of my life has been the fact that neither of my parents lived long enough to share in what I've been able to accomplish in the last 20 years or so. My mom passed away in '72 and my dad followed two years later. Both were 56 years old. To this day, I still miss them. I'll always miss them.*

"*So please don't let your pride or your downright stubbornness or anything else come between you and your kids. Enjoy them. Love them. And please, dads, give 'em all a big hug Sunday.*

"*You'll feel like a million bucks.*"

—TERRY BOERS. *DAILY HERALD*
(LISLE, ILL.: 16 JUNE 1995), SEC. 2, P. 2.

grandkids, especially the achievements and successes. While these proud parents might feel a little self-conscious informing friends and neighbors (and even siblings) about the latest test score, home run, recital, and award, bragging to grandparents is accepted and even expected.

Jeff R. explains that his father died when his three girls were very young. So his dad missed all of their junior-high, high-school, and now college experiences. Jeff admits, "I guess I feel the loss most often at my daughters' sporting events. I also miss Dad at other big moments such as weddings because I know he won't be there when my girls get married."

"I wish my dad could see my kids!" Mike S. exclaims. "He'd be so proud of them. I guess that's when I miss Dad the most, when my kids are performing, because I know he would get so much joy."

Those feelings are echoed by Jeff B. He says, "Recently I've felt Dad's absence even more as the boys are growing up. I keep thinking, *I wish Dad knew about this*. I'd love to share their accomplishments with him. I miss the joy. I feel this loss of the undivided audience."

These men wish they could tell their dads about his grandkids and long for that appreciative ear that always welcomed their statements as proud fathers. But the audience is gone.

PARENTING PASSAGES

The long, winding parenting journey begins before birth, as a couple prays, plans, and prepares. Usually their parents, the expected baby's grandparents, are not too involved in the process yet. But that changes at birth, and the interaction usually increases along the way.

For the new mom and dad, each stage of parenting comes with the realization that this has been done before, only we were on the receiving end. That is, we parents are following in our parents' footsteps. When through drowsy eyes we try to rock our infants to sleep at 2 A.M., we think of the sleepless nights our mothers and fathers experienced because of us as newborns. As we try to interest the child in a Gerber meal and, instead, get a face full of strained peas for our efforts, we wonder how Dad did it, how he kept his cool under that pressure. And as we celebrate each milestone of maturity for our children, we think of what our parents must have thought when they experienced the same with us—how Dad must have felt when he first heard "Daddy!"

"In the middle of a joyous World Series celebration on the field, Paul O'Neill hugged his manager and wept. O'Neill's father had died earlier Wednesday after a long struggle with heart problems, and Joe Torre had a special message for his right fielder.

"'Your dad got to watch this one,' Torre told O'Neill.

"Then, O'Neill jogged off the field, wiping his eyes as he entered the dugout, no longer able to control his emotions. 'It obviously came out at the end,' O'Neill said. He broke down again in the clubhouse.

"'I'm proud to be here. I'm proud to be part of this team . . . but believe me, I lost someone special,' he said, his voice cracking."

—ASSOCIATED PRESS. AS QUOTED ON WWW.ESPN.COM.

Then sending a child to school, struggling through early adolescence, helping the child move toward independence during high school, and sending the child to college—at each stage, we gain a fresh appreciation for what our parents must have endured, especially Dad as we follow in his footsteps. During the early parenting passages, you could discuss each challenge with your father, thank him and your mother for what they had done for you, ask for his insights and what to expect at the next stage, and find camaraderie through his stories. You could talk with Dad about what it took to be a good father. With him gone, however, you are left with memories of his fathering example and can only hope that somehow he knows your gratitude. And wouldn't it be great if you could ask him how he dealt with his father's death?

Paul V., reflecting on his relationship with his father, says, "I wish Dad could have been around to see his grandchildren grow up. I would have liked for him to be proud of me as a father as he saw how good my kids have turned out. He was not able to see that, and I regret that. Sometimes I feel as though I was never quite good enough or that he was somewhat disappointed with me, so I feel that if he had seen my family grow up, it would have erased that. I wish I had the maturity I have now back then; however, some maturation only comes through life experiences. So I wish Dad could be around today and see my family and me. I think he would be pleasantly surprised."

Ralph remembers a particularly poignant time with his father. In the middle of his freshman year of college, Ralph was about to go overseas for a three-month mission trip. He says, "Dad pulled me aside and said, 'I think we ought to pray together before you go.' He started to pray and then broke down and cried. I had not seen Dad cry before. This was a bonding experience that I had never experienced with him. Now I've gone through similar experiences with my kids, and I'd love to compare notes with Dad. He'd understand."

Facing the daily challenges of being a good husband and father, a son also gains an appreciation of the sacrifices that his father made to support the family. Most of the men we interviewed described their fathers as keeping most of their feelings inside or, at least, not exposing them to the children. So as they were growing up, these sons knew little about financial crises, conflicts at work, and spiritual journeys. Yet each of these sons has faced some of those experiences and would love the opportunity to talk them over with his dad. But it's too late.

"When my parents dropped me off at college, with tears brimming in his eyes and poised to roll down his cheeks, Dad told me that I was a good son and thanked me for setting a positive example for my three younger brothers. Then he slipped behind the wheel of our Pontiac station wagon, next to Mom, and drove away. I didn't fully understand the emotional trauma of that moment until Gail and I took Kara to her college and left her there. I wish Dad and I could discuss our common experience."

—DAVE VEERMAN

COUNSEL

In addition to parenting concerns, we men have many other areas in which we need counsel and advice. Dads seem to know everything, especially to a young child. And every father has a special area of knowledge and expertise beyond his vocation—finance, carpentry, auto mechanics, gardening, woodworking, food preparation, music, and so forth. For so many years, we take that knowledge for granted.

Dick E. remembers driving home from a trip when his car just quit running. He says, "It started knocking or something. I had no idea what was wrong with it, but I pulled over. In fact, I don't even know if we ever went back to get the car. But I called Dad. He came and picked us up and took us home. Then he and I went out and bought a car. My wife didn't appreciate it very much because I bought it without her seeing it. But my dad said the car was OK, so it was OK. I didn't call him that much for help, but it was just that I knew he was there when I needed him. He would know what to do."

Mike S. can identify with Dick's loss. He says, "The person who I could go to for advice was gone. I didn't have a relationship with anyone else like that."

"At 82, my father still went to the office every day," says Marshall, a Bible publisher from Indiana. "Working with him I had time to prepare for his death because I knew that every day could be his last. I was very prepared. And knowing where Dad was, I was at peace. I miss Dad the most when there's a critical business decision to make. We weren't just father and son—we were partners."

And Harry adds, "I miss my father the most when I'm working on projects around the house and need to ask for his advice."

Fathers also have wisdom from years of living, having experienced the highs and lows of life and having learned from their successes and failures. As we sons are growing up, however, we don't often ask for our fathers' counsel, or we don't take their advice. Consequently, we make our own mistakes. Then, when it's too late, we wish we could have their invaluable help. Mike B., an executive with YMCA, says, "My dad was always supportive of me and found the time to do a lot things with me, especially outdoors. Since my father's death, I haven't replaced the confidante he was to me. When it comes to listening to me, nobody has ever taken Dad's place."

Although Ray H. admits to not being very close to his father, he says, "Thirty-two years after my father's death, I still long to pick up the phone and be able to talk to him. Nobody can take the place of a person's father."

It also stands true that no one knows a boy as well as his father does. Parents understand their children because they have known the kids all of their young lives. Mom and Dad witness the ups, downs, and in-betweens, and they see the attitudes and aptitudes and the desires and dreams. In a family of boys, the sons will differ from each other greatly, but they all will be like their father. As we have already discussed, this "dad-ness" emerges especially in values, in attitudes toward church, money, family, and work. The father is reflected in his sons, if not in their appearance then in their values, actions, senses of humor, and parenting styles. Knowing him so well, then, a father would certainly be able to advise his son in his decisions. But he's not available anymore to answer questions and to offer his counsel and guidance.

Phil V. says, "One of my biggest disappointments is that Dad is not here to steer me or my kids. Dad and Mom were always supportive, and not having them here hurts. I was always recognized when my father was alive. I long for his recognition and approval."

Al regrets that he did not have his father later on in life so that he could ask his father's opinions about how to build a house and about finances. Jeff R. says he misses being able to call his dad for advice. Tom E. simply says, "It would be fun to call him once in a while. He was an investment broker, and I wonder what he'd say about the stock market these days and how I should respond."

Kurt, a consultant for a business services company, says, "I never realized how much I missed my dad until I needed him for advice and was forced to accept the fact that he wasn't there. When I was ready to get engaged, I wanted certainty, and I needed to talk to my dad about it. Since Dad got married at forty, I figured he'd be able to help me process my fears and doubts. But he wasn't there."

We miss Dad—our most supportive and devoted fan.

DOUBLE LOSS

Neglected sons also feel this loss very early in life and may spend years trying to get their fathers' attention and approval. Their actions seem to say, "Maybe someday Dad will appreciate me!" When that kind of father dies, the son may have the almost overwhelming sensation of *unfinished business* and feel deep regret and even anger.

"You cannot go through the holidays without seeing at least a dozen movies that remind you of a positive father/son relationship. I never had a Christmas with my own father. Not just during the holidays but probably a hundred times a year something makes me wish I would have had a relationship with my dad. But that's where you have to again say, thank you, Lord, for the great mom you gave me. Thank you for my brothers. Thank you for the man who led me to Christ and was a mentor to me. And thank you most of all again that you're a God who is a father to the fatherless."

—DR. JOHN TRENT

Tragically, many fathers are just plain bad. Abusive or absent, they inflict great injury on their children. And then there are those boys who lose their fathers at a young age. With the death of these fathers, adult sons, even Christian men, may be confused about their feelings and may mourn the loss of "Daddy" and the loving audience that they never had.

- Bill K. says, "I felt the loss of not having a father to teach me about manhood and fatherhood and relationships. It left an empty spot in my life."

- Phil M. explains, "When my father died, I lost the role model of how to deal with my children. Because I was 13 when he died, I do not know how to deal with a 13+-year-old boy or girl. I didn't get to see my father do that."

- Cap, an industrial chemical salesman from California, was 56 when his father died at the age of 83. Although he loved his dad, Cap says he struggled with his father continuing to treat him as a child and not as an adult peer. This strained their relationship. Cap withdrew from his father in order to not feel "controlled," but that kept his own kids from having time with their grandfather. He says, "I miss my dad. I regret that we were never able to establish a complete adult relationship, and it cost all of us family time together."

- Ed, a university professor, was 47 when his father died at 77. Ed never felt close to his father and can't recall his father ever saying he loved him. But just prior to his father's death, Ed received a letter from his dad in which he acknowledged Ed's expression of love. He ended the letter by saying, "I love you too." That letter is so precious to Ed that he keeps it in a lock box at his bank and looks at it often. Eight years after his father's death, Ed sat down and wrote out a letter to his dad attempting to bring closure to a less-than-satisfying relationship.

- "I hated my father," admits Bill J. Bill had worked hard at staying in touch with his dad over the years. (His mom and dad divorced when Bill was just four years old.) He finally made peace with his father during his senior year at college, at a gathering of Christian students. He explains, "One night, I stood and confessed that I hated my father and that I could finally release him in forgiveness. I realized that he was just a guy like me, and I could have compassion for him." Bill also had wrestled with his view of God, and he adds, "I began to stop blaming God."

SEEING GOD AS FATHER

The good news is that God can fill that father void. In fact, Scripture speaks continually of God as "Father." The Apostle Paul declares, "For this reason I kneel before the Father, from whom his whole family in heaven and on earth derives its name" (Eph. 3:14–15 NIV). Quite naturally, we tend to project our ideas of fatherhood on God because our first understanding of the nature and duties of a father comes from our earthly fathers. Thus many people perceive God in negative terms, especially those whose fathers deserted the family or who were unpredictable and violent. They may think, *If God is like my father, then I certainly don't want anything to do with him.*

For example, Ray K. says, "I never heard Dad say anything positive to me. No word of affirmation and praise for what I had done. No comment on my character. So it was a big jump from that to my 'heavenly Father.' On the twenty-fifth anniversary of my father's death, I returned to the gravesite, and I prayed, 'Lord, why did you take him?' But then I thought, 'I wouldn't be as close to you, Lord, if you hadn't.' It was then that I was able to transcend my feelings, and God really became my dad."

So many of the guys we interviewed had dads who were World War II vintage. These fathers were workaholics, and many were silent. None of them, of course, had ever read an article on how to be a better father or how to reveal your feelings. Think of how much material we have today—books, videos, magazines, seminars—and back then they had nothing. A father was a provider. He wasn't running around with other women, he brought a paycheck home to his wife, and he kept his house in good shape. He did everything he was supposed to do. Anything more was unheard of.

Yet as a teenager, I felt that I didn't have the father I thought I needed. For years I tried to make God my father and sought that relationship earnestly in prayer. While doing these interviews, however, I realized that I have been resisting the role that my father had in conveying to me what God was like. I've been trying to go straight to God theologically. But God doesn't have a physical body, so he can't take me fishing and he can't hug me when I feel bad. As I thought about the qualities of God that my father did portray—wisdom, forethought, watchfulness, integrity, and honesty—and thanked God for those qualities in him, things began to open up for me.

Nobody has a perfect father, but nearly all the men we talked to pointed to qualities in their fathers that could be seen as attributes of God. By regarding and accepting the father I had, I was better able to experience the love of God. (Bruce Barton)

God, "our Father in heaven" (Matthew 6:9), models all of the ideal qualities of a good father: loving, compassionate, present, kind, and just. God provides and leads; he corrects and disciplines. He cares for his children and is always available to listen to them and to guide them.

Regardless of the quality of our experience with our earthly fathers, therefore, we can run to our heavenly Father, calling him "Daddy" and pouring out our hearts to him. Paul reminds us, "So you should not be like cowering, fearful slaves. You should behave instead like God's very own children, adopted into his family—calling him 'Father, dear Father'" (Romans 8:15). "God has sent the Spirit of his Son into your hearts, and now you can call God your dear Father" (Galatians 4:6).

Even after our earthly fathers are gone, we can talk to God about anything, telling him about our accomplishments, bragging about our kids, and asking for his divine counsel.

"Pray like this: Our Father in heaven, may your name be honored" (Matthew 6:9).

"If you sinful people know how to give good gifts to your children, how much more will your heavenly Father give good gifts to those who ask him" (Matthew 7:11).

"May God our Father and the Lord Jesus Christ give you his grace and peace" (1 Corinthians 1:3).

"All praise to the God and Father of our Lord Jesus Christ. He is the source of every mercy and the God who comforts us" (2 Corinthians 1:3).

"There is only one God and Father, who is over us all and in us all and living through us all" (Ephesians 4:6).

"And you will always give thanks for everything to God the Father in the name of our Lord Jesus Christ" (Ephesians 5:20).

"All honor to the God and Father of our Lord Jesus Christ, for it is by his boundless mercy that God has given us the privilege of being born again. Now we live with a wonderful expectation because Jesus Christ rose again from the dead" (1 Peter 1:3).

"See how very much our heavenly Father loves us, for he allows us to be called his children, and we really are! But the people who belong to this world don't know God, so they don't understand that we are his children" (1 John 3:1).

BUILDING MEMORIES

Dads play a critical role with their children, especially their sons. Even poor or absent fathers make a significant impact. We need to be aware, therefore, that our actions *today* will be remembered *tomorrow*. In other words, even if our kids seem to

---

"When my father died, I recalled so much of what he had accomplished after coming to Christ. That happened when I was just a boy. Our family was the 'lost' back then. We were the un-churched and un-reached. But the death of my baby brother, the only other child in the family, brought my dad to such terrible grief that it drove him to take his remaining son to church, and that's where I found Christ. Dad would just sit out in the car and wait for me. One Sunday, a man came out and said to him, 'I teach the men's Sunday school class, and I'd love to have you come.'

"Dad answered, 'Naw, naw. I wouldn't have the clothes for that.'

"I thank God that the man said, 'It doesn't matter how you dress, that's fine.' So the following Sunday my dad came into church. Later, on Christmas Eve, he came forward and gave his heart to Christ, and that's how I know he's in heaven today.

"Over the years, that memory and very personal experience has motivated me to go to the lost and reach them where they are, which is usually outside the walls of the church. That's where somebody had to go to reach my dad. Had they waited for him to come in, I don't know if he would be in heaven today."

—RON HUTCHCRAFT

---

be taking us for granted, we can be confident that our presence and involvement are making strong impressions.

Many sons feel the loss of audience most acutely because their fathers exerted a major, positive force in their lives. When they think of "Dad," they have positive, warm memories. So consider this: After you are gone, how will your children, especially your sons, remember you? At your funeral, what image of you will your kids share?

Make the most of the living years.

BEING A MENTOR

Understanding the impact, for good or bad, that our fathers have had on us can motivate us to be significant adults in the lives of children whose fathers have died or deserted them.

Every community has programs that offer responsible and mature men the opportunity to link up with young boys who don't have fathers. You don't need a formal program, however, to befriend a neighbor, relative, or young person at church. You will discover many opportunities to show love and to provide a positive male image to boys who need dads. You can make a difference, helping a boy become a man.

Throughout Scripture, the "fatherless" (along with "widows") are singled out for special consideration and concern. God cares for children who have no fathers, and so should we.

Suddenly having no one to cheer us on, appreciate our achievements,

> *"Pure and lasting religion in the sight of God our Father means that we must care for orphans and widows in their troubles, and refuse to let the world corrupt us"* (James 1:27).

listen to our complaints, and offer us counsel can be devastating. We can no longer turn and call out, "Daddy, watch me!" We see that the audience has left. But we can learn from this experience—seeing God as Father, building memories with our children, and being mentors and surrogate fathers to the fatherless.

WHAT DO YOU THINK?

1. When you were growing up, how did your father demonstrate that he was your biggest fan?

2. In what ways was your father a positive audience? In what ways was he a negative audience?

3. What do you miss most about losing your father as your audience?

4. What helps you relate to God as your Father?

5. What will you change in your priorities and schedule in order to become more involved in your children's lives, to become a positive audience and influence?

6. What fatherless kids do you know?

7. What will you do to befriend or mentor a fatherless child?

7

POWERSHIFT

Receiving the Mantle

Group dynamics change as quickly as the members of the group. We've all experienced those moments when the mood in a room changes unexpectedly, instantly.

A girl walks into a party, and the packed room seems to fall suddenly silent . . .

A guy stands just outside his school, waiting for the bell to ring. Smiling and relaxed, he jokes and laughs with a circle of friends . . . until *the new guy* arrives, turning the attention to himself . . .

The younger brother and sister get along just fine. But whenever the older brother appears, tension builds between the younger two . . .

Any chemistry student knows that the smallest changes in a chemical formula or compound can lead to drastic and even deadly consequences. The formula for carbon dioxide, for example, is CO_2; that is, each molecule consists of one atom of carbon and two atoms of oxygen. All living things enjoy an intimate relationship with this compound—without it we could not live. Animals exhale it, and plants take it in. Removing just one atom of oxygen, however, results in carbon monoxide, a deadly gas. The composition makes all the difference. It's a matter of chemistry.

Similar reactions occur in human relationships. Certain combinations work, and others just don't mix very well. It's true in pairs and in groups. Thus, we talk about the "chemistry" of a team, a class, a community, a Bible study, or a dating couple.

So why should a family be different? Change the ingredients, and you change the chemistry. Remember your freshman year in college when you came home for Christmas break? You probably expected to move smoothly back into your role and status in the family. But it wasn't very smooth; in fact, your younger brother or sister seemed annoyed and at times downright hostile. That's because the chemistry had changed, and you were now encroaching into your brother or sister's territory. This happens in families every time major change occurs: a newborn or adopted child arrives, a son or daughter gets married, an older child returns to live at home for a while, parents divorce. In each occasion, the family is reconstituted, reformulated, and the members must adjust. It's not the same as before.

So imagine the cataclysmic change brought by the death of a father!

CHANGING ROLES

The first abrupt change, felt almost immediately by the whole clan and especially the surviving sons, concerns Dad's place in the family. Who will assume his position? Who will take his role? That's what happened with John D. He explains, "Ours was a very patriarchal family. So as the oldest son, I felt responsibility to take my father's place, to be the family leader. That was difficult."

Spike was *not* the oldest child, but he remembers jumping into his father's place. He says, "My mother was in a trance. My sister was in shock. My brother didn't say a word. I had to take charge."

An automobile accident abruptly ended Red's life. His son, Dick, was a young man at the time, about 30 years old. He says, "I felt responsible. I no longer had Dad to turn to, so I had to step up, to measure up. That became the recurring theme of my life—measuring up, doing what's right—and it really started then. Decisions had to be made. We had to decide, for instance, what we should do about the guy who had hit him. Should we sue? I had to deal with those matters. I suddenly felt responsibility at a different level. I grew up."

For many men, the father's death becomes a catalyst, a motivating force. Jim F. recalls, "It drove me to work harder. I became to *my* family what my dad had been to our family."

For Phil V., this sad event became part of his spiritual renewal. He explains, "Dad's death timed with my recommitment to Christ and totally flipped my life. Not only did Christ become the focal point in my life, but also my family and my time with my family. I wasn't driven by work anymore."

Adjusting Relationships

The relational dynamics in the family also change. Sometimes those changes are positive and good; sometimes they're difficult and frustrating.

Phil V. says, "Dad was the communication link among all of our family members because we were so spread out. His death was a broken link. So we have had to work to stay in touch."

"Dad's death brought my brothers and me closer," says Bill W. "And Mom became more open. She had been like Dad, keeping her thoughts and feelings hidden. But after Dad's death, she just unloaded. Now we talk every day."

Jim W. had a similar experience concerning his mother. He says, "My father's death had a liberating effect on Mom. She really came into her own. She lived thirteen more years, during

"The father is never more than 10 digits away, and when Joe Buck gets desperate for the sound of his old man's voice, he dials Jack's cell phone so he can hear the rasp that entertained St. Louis Cardinals fans—and national TV and radio audiences—for nearly half a century. 'I always gave him a hug and a kiss on the cheek whenever I saw him,' says Joe, reminiscing about his father, who died after a lengthy illness on June 18. 'I loved him so much, and I showed that a lot' . . .

"The night that Jack died, Joe was where his dad would have expected him to be: broadcasting the Cardinals' game against the Anaheim Angels at Busch Stadium. Afterward, he drove to St. Louis's Barnes-Jewish Hospital for a farewell. 'They had taken him off the respirator [earlier that evening], and I knew it was a matter of time,' says Joe. 'His breathing had slowed, and I didn't know if he was still breathing. I leaned in and talked in his ear for about 50 seconds before leaving the room. I never looked back. I didn't want to be there like in some movie ending when a father takes his last breath, because I know what he would have said: 'Get out of here, kid.'

"Jack died about 20 minutes later, and if you ask Ann, she's sure it went according to Jack's plan. 'It's like his dad was waiting for him,' she says softly. 'All of us believe that Jack waited to see Joe one more time before he passed away.'"

—RICHARD DEITSCH. "A SHINING SON." SPORTS
ILLUSTRATED (OCTOBER 28, 2002), 38.

which she traveled more, became more involved in church and with other people, and spent time with the grandchildren."

John D. explains, "I saw our family begin to pull together.

Because of our upbringing and age gaps, we had never been close. But this was the beginning. For example, my brother-in-law became more involved in the family."

But many changes are not nearly so encouraging, involving relational conflicts and even family splits.

One man reported that a few months after his father's death, he and his sister were discussing their younger brother. They were deeply concerned that he had been making some self-destructive lifestyle choices, and they decided to confront him, together, about the issue. During the confrontation, the younger brother became defensive and then angry, and he shouted, "Who do you think you are? You're not my father!" Ironically, the young man probably would not have listened to his father's counsel either. But he was declaring that his siblings had no right to step into his father's role and try to direct his life, even though their actions were motivated by love.

Though with different issues, a similar scene played out with Phil M. He explains, "Dad was sick in the winter, and he died in the spring. In the fall, my next oldest brother went to college. (The others were already gone.) So in eighth grade, I was the man of the house. My older brothers tried to take a bigger role in my life. When they were nurturing, it was fine. But I found myself saying, 'You're not my father!' Dad had been the disciplinarian, and Mom had been the nurturer. Because I was 13, Mom had to become, almost instantly, the heavy-handed disciplinarian in the house. So instead of being the nurturing mother, she became the hard-nosed parent. So, in effect, when I lost my father, I lost my mother. In college, I remember a friend telling me, 'You strike me as someone who had to grow up too soon.'"

A family with several siblings had a meeting to discuss their parents' possessions and other related issues. (The mother had passed away two years prior to their father's death.) "It felt very awkward," reports one of the brothers. "Everyone just sat there and made suggestions, but no one wanted to take the lead. I guess we all were afraid of what the others would think. It took forever to make a decision on even the smallest matter."

In another family, one of the brothers insisted on being the leader. His actions were resented by his siblings and his mother and eventually caused a split in the family. A younger brother explains, "Even though Dad died several years ago, I still can't talk to my brother. He's always trying to tell me what to do, to control my life!"

"I was also troubled by a dream I'd just had. In it, I'd forgotten the sound of my own father's voice. I woke up in a fierce sweat and realized I'd been weeping. Unable to go back to sleep, I sat in a chair by the window, struck by the powerful reality that I would never again be able simply to pick up the phone and call my father and hear him laugh and say he was going to pin my ears back. I remember sitting in that chair thinking I was no longer a son."

—JAMES DODSON. FINAL ROUNDS: A FATHER, A SON, THE GOLF JOURNEY OF A LIFETIME (NEW YORK: BANTAM BOOKS, 1997), 251–52.

Bill J. tells of caring for his ailing father for several years and eventually moving him to a nursing home in the same town so they could be close. His parents had divorced decades earlier, but Bill had tried to stay in touch with his father over the years. During the last months of the father's life, Bill had invested countless hours in visiting, making decisions, and organizing the father's affairs. And when his father died, Bill took care of the funeral arrangements. Despite all this, Bill's two sisters, who both lived several states away, gave him a hard time. He says, "They guilt-tripped me. They said I hadn't done enough."

Family dynamics can be complex, involving patterns of actions and reactions learned from years of living together. Thus, changes in family chemistry can evoke volatile reactions.

CARING FOR MOM

Many of the new family decisions involve the surviving mother, especially if she has been very dependent on her husband. A son's relationship with his mom can change dramatically.

"Dad's death had a big effect on my relationship with Mom," recalls Jeff R. "Her security blanket, Dad, had been ripped away, so she struggled big time. Eventually she saw that life goes on. I needed to be more confrontational, taking on more of a peer role, an advisor role."

Len was a teenager when his father died, so his mother was young as well. He says, "How did my dad's death affect my relationship with my mom? I felt very protective of her. Dad had been a great husband. None of us has any doubt that Mom was his top priority. Many days Dad would come home from work around supper time, and Mom would say, 'I'll buy you a cup of coffee.' Then she would pour a cup, and they would go back in their bedroom and review the events of the day. It was like he wanted to see her first, visit with her, and catch up on things. After five or ten minutes, they would come out, and we would have supper. Mom was devastated when Dad died, and I felt protective. But I also felt kind of impotent to really help her."

Len remembers a special time with his mom. He says, "When the Jazz basketball team was still in New Orleans, I took Mom on a date to a game. It's kind of like giving your mother a football for

Christmas, but she talks about that to this day. It was just a real special memory for her that I spent my money on the tickets. We went to Sizzler Steakhouse beforehand or whatever, and I drove her across the lake and everything. That was a fun memory."

"An emotional roller coaster" is how Mike S. describes his mother's reactions to his father's death. "She had been so dependent on Dad, and she needed me. So I found myself driving back to her house constantly. I had to take care of her and help her through the process."

Roger's mother was older when his father died. He says, "I realized that I had to be the caretaker at that point. I had to step in and take care of Mom. I checked in regularly, with more intentional care. I would try to talk with her about her feelings."

John D. says, "Dad's death reminded me of Mom's mortality. The way I treated her changed immediately—calls, visits, especially the last year or two. We hadn't shown much emotion as a family, but we cried together too. It was good for both of us. And Mom's a 'hugger' now."

The relationship with Mom can change dramatically, with her needs overshadowing ours. She now needs us more than we need her. This is especially true for a mother who has leaned heavily upon her husband through the years. His death can leave her feeling desperately alone and lost. This woman's children may not have known the extent of their mother's dependence on their father—she always seemed to be in control and able to meet their needs, even into adulthood. So these adult children now see Mom in a new light, and they are forced to change their expectations and actions. It's a profound shift.

Becoming a Man

Another dynamic change occurs on a much more personal level. Men use a variety of phrases to describe this change, this rite of passage. Certainly the heightened sense of one's own mortality, realization of the quick passing of time, and the assumption of new roles and responsibilities all contribute to this feeling. But other factors heighten this sudden move toward maturity.

"Although I was 26 years old, I entered manhood in a new way as I watched my father die," says Paul T., a publisher from Michigan. "Dad was a faithful Christian who had faced a long bout with lung cancer heroically, using it as an extended opportunity to talk to others about eternal matters and to plant in them new seeds of joy and hope."

This example of courage and faith became a life-changing event for Paul. He continues, "The tremendously energetic faith in Jesus Christ with which Dad faced the whole struggle seemed to gather together at the last, as he lay dying, into a lightning bolt of spiritual power that struck me and transformed me as he slipped away to the Father. That day, my attitude toward death and eternity was changed forever. It's as if, now that his faith had at last given way to sight and he no longer needed it, he passed it on to me. It was his last, best gift to me on this earth."

> "It has been said that a man is not a man until his father is gone. If this was what manhood felt like, I had real questions about whether I was up to it."
>
> —JOHN ASHCROFT. LESSONS FROM A FATHER TO A SON (NASHVILLE, TENN.: THOMAS NELSON PUBLISHERS, 1998), 201.

Edwin, himself a WWII veteran and a retired pastor from Washington, reports that the reality of his father's death caused him to look more deeply into the Scriptures—for himself, not just to find sermon outlines. "As a result of the Bible becoming more alive," he says, "I became a stronger Christian and a more mature individual." Indirectly, his father's passing triggered that personal growth.

Some men described the feeling as one of being delegated new responsibilities and authority. Paul V. reflects this when he says, "I felt that a page had been turned in my life, and the cycle was complete. The 'baton' had been passed to me. I no longer could be considered the son. I was now fully the father and had to take on the mantle that the title held. I don't think my behavior changed much, but the emotion did change. It was a sad feeling but a necessary passage for me."

For many, this change came much too soon, well before normal "adulthood." John B., a motivational speaker from Illinois, explains that his dad died on their family vacation. John was 13, and his dad was 56. Given John's age and the fact that his two older brothers were on their own, John says, "This traumatic event thrust me into instant manhood. There I was, just a kid, yet the man of the house. I wondered what I should do now."

This can bring a host of problems and pressures. Bill K. says, "Although I was only about 14 when my father died, in many ways, that's when I became a man. But not having his example or role model for so many years, I wonder, at times, what I should be as a man and as a father. And I wish I knew better how to relate to men."

A father's death pulls his son up to a new level of maturity and responsibility. The boy becomes a man.

FINDING A FATHER

We have seen how a father's death alters the family chemistry. Roles change and relationships adjust. Dad's chair sits empty. Sons of any age, but usually those who are young, often seek to fill that space, seeking to learn more about their father and to find others to assume that role. For example, the sudden death of the father means that the son, especially a young son, loses his role model and his authority figure. Often the boy will then sift through memories and memoirs to learn more about his father.

To My Father, on the First Anniversary of His Passing

A year ago today I stood and wept beside your bed.
The veil was rent, and through that tear I caught a glimpse
    of glory:
I saw you crush the mocking Serpent underneath your heel.
I saw you drop the weary rags and don the shining robe.
I saw you laugh at fear and trade your trial for a crown.
I saw you greet the Shepherd and lie down beside His stream.
So many gifts you gave me, but the last by far was best:
A year ago, on your deathbed, your son was new-begotten.
My grief gave way to courage then
and I became a man.

—DR. PAUL THIGPEN

Len says, "I don't know how to say this and be very eloquent, but I think in some regard, that I spent the next ten years of my life, from eighteen until I got married, at twenty-eight, looking for my father. I was searching for my heavenly Father, but, at the same time, I was trying to figure out who my dad was. I didn't feel like I really knew him that well. I remember asking a lot of questions and being intrigued anytime I would find an old picture or some artifact from the War or whatever. Those things were special to me because they were a small clue into the true identity of the man who brought me into the world."

The young son also may seek, subconsciously, a man to take his father's place. Len continues, "Interestingly enough, just before I went off to college, my mother remarried. And the man she married had been my dad's friend in college. My mom, this man, Jack, and my father had all been part of the same group, and they had remained friends through the years. About a year after my dad died with cancer, Jack's wife died, also from cancer. She had been struggling with it for years. So my mom and this male friend from her college days ended up together. It seems strange, now because I've known my step-dad, Jack, longer than I knew my dad. For twenty-six years he has been my step-dad, so he has been the father figure in my life. I was almost an adult when he came into my life, so we related more as peers, but he is somebody I treasure and enjoy being with, solicit advice from, and bounce ideas off."

Len says he feels "super-blessed," having enjoyed two fathers. He explains, "Jack has been a terrific granddad to my boys, just adores my wife, and takes care of my mom. But it's funny. I have this picture of Jack, my step-dad, and my dad at a church picnic with their arms around each other, holding a softball bat in their hands. The picture was taken before either one of them had ever been married, before my mom was even in the picture. That's a real treasure to me."

Some men explained that a youth leader or family friend filled the father role, providing a positive role model for faith, relationships, and manhood.

Many men who were in their forties or fifties when their fathers died, and regardless of the quality of their father-son relationship, spoke of needing and finding a new mentor, an older man. This friend provides answers, guidance, and counsel. He has been there before. He knows the way through.

I didn't realize what I was looking for, at first. But soon after my dad died, I began to crave the fellowship of men. I got in touch with my uncles, and joined a men's group at church. The ultimate fellowship group was our family's men's weekend. My father-in-law had one son and five daughters, so he, his son, and all four sons-in-law went fishing for a weekend in Cape May, New Jersey. During that weekend we talked about our dads (three of us had fathers who had passed away) and how we would spend time together if they could come back for a day. We talked for hours. This men's weekend has become a tradition that we've kept for nine years. Now my three boys and son-in-law come, giving us a total of twelve men. It has become a great way for all of us to connect. (Bruce Barton)

If you feel this longing, think of who might fill that role for you—perhaps a favorite uncle, a father-in-law, a pastor, or a man at church.

BREAKING THE CYCLE

The "power shift" often means that the son feels enormous pressure to now take Dad's place in the family. This isn't necessarily bad, but it can feel almost devastating in a dysfunctional family.

Children tend to become like their parents. Many of the similarities are positive and healthy, and some are rather innocuous. But we also tend to repeat our father's bad habits. And that's not good. When a father dies, therefore, the son can feel as though he is doomed to be just like his abusive role model. He isn't "doomed," of course, but it will take concerted effort to be different, to break the cycle.

Breaking the cycle may simply mean changing patterns of relating to our children. Coming from a family in which outward displays of affection were nonexistent, a son can work on hugging his wife and kids and verbally expressing his love for them. And a son who is tempted to follow his father's pattern of withholding approval and giving only words of condemnation will have to work hard at being positive and affirming. Breaking negative behavioral patterns must be intentional.

"I didn't want my daughters to remember my father as somebody who was never there, a shadow, a cipher. So I took his decorations from World War II, the Purple Heart with three clusters, the Silver Star, the Bronze Star that he received, the Pacific service ribbons, the Blue Combat Infantryman Badge, all of that and his little Eisenhower cap that the men wore, and I had a framer put everything in a shadowbox. I wanted to highlight these mementos of that time in my dad's life when he was heroic, when he served our country with honor. And guess what? If you come to our home today, the box sits above the piano where my daughters practice their piano lessons. All they have to do is just look up and they see the flag—I have it mounted as well—that we got when he passed away. There's a Samurai sword that he brought back from Guadalcanal. And then there's the shadowbox of all my dad's military decorations because, again, I want them to remember Grandpa at his best."

—Dr. John Trent

My dad was hardworking, intense, quiet, and distant. Though he was home every night, he kept his thoughts and feelings to himself. I determined to be different, to spend time interacting with my kids. But it takes some sacrifice to listen when you don't feel like it, to hang out when you've got stuff to do. I ended up coaching two of my sons' soccer teams for six years and watching hundreds of games. And the rides in the car and stops for hamburgers helped build the kind of strong relationship with my boys that I wish I had had with my father. (Bruce Barton)

Some of these parenting patterns can be much more extreme

and problematic—fathers who are almost totally absent, emotionally distant, or abusive. Tragically, those cycles are often repeated in the sons, with terrible results. Studies consistently show that alcoholic fathers tend to produce alcoholic sons and that abusive fathers often were themselves abused as children. We tend to absorb the values that have been modeled for us and to follow the lifestyles that we have observed in our homes. This is a formula that must be changed, or we'll perpetuate the chain reaction.

"One kind of relationship that almost never gets worse after the death of a father is that between the surviving son and his children. Among the 181 men in our survey who had children at the time their fathers died, none said that their connections with their children worsened in the two years after the death. Meanwhile, more than a quarter of these men—26 percent—said their relationships with their children improved.

"Often, the improvements came when the bereaved son reexamined his relationship with his father. After such review, the son would make a conscious decision about how to parent his own children in response to the way he'd been raised by his father."

—Neil Chethik. *FatherLoss*
(New York: Hyperion, 2001), 205.

Ray K., himself a professional counselor, relates, "As my children have gotten older, I have been able to share my feelings about not having a dad. I've seen the alcoholic pattern up close.

In fact, we three brothers are the only males on my father's side of the family without an addiction problem. We all have been determined to break the cycle."

This has not been easy. Ray continues, "From my father, I learned much of what not to do, and I saw what happens in a family without a man at the helm. I continue to shadowbox against those patterns, those tendencies. I had to accept what I didn't get and deal with it. I had no fathering model. When you live in an alcoholic family, it burns out your senses. Either you learn to manage the pain and grow, or you give in to the addictions and other problems."

Several groups provide help to people with similar histories. "Adult Children of Alcoholics" is one. And professional counselors can provide priceless help for overcoming the odds and breaking the cycle of dominance or addiction or abuse. Just because the father has died does not mean that the son is freed from his influence. For better or worse, we carry our fathers with us. So if you need help, get it.

Through all of these changes in chemistry we can be confident that Christ is with us always (Matthew 28:20), changing us from the inside (2 Corinthians 5:17), and helping us want to obey him and then do what he wants (Philippians 2:13). With God's help, we can break the negative cycles. As Moses declares, "Satisfy us in the morning with your unfailing love, so we may sing for joy to the end of our lives. Give us gladness in proportion to our former misery! Replace the evil years with good. Let us see your miracles again; let our children see your glory at work" (Psalm 90:14–16).

A father's death changes the chemistry of a family. The boy becomes a man, the care receiver becomes the caregiver, the child becomes the father, and the family is redefined.

WHAT DO YOU THINK?

1. How did your father's death change your family's chemistry?

2. Who assumed your father's place in the family? How did that make you feel?

3. After your father died, how did your family relationships change positively? Negatively?

4. If your mother survived your father, how did she react to his death? In what ways did your relationship with her change?

5. How do you react to the statement, "A man is not a man until his father is gone"?

6. In what ways did your father's death affect your relationships with other men?

7. What have you done to break the negative cycles in your past, regarding your father? What can you do?

8

OVER THE SHOULDER
Charting Our Own Course

"You can do it!" Justin encourages as he holds the back of the seat and helps steer the bike down the driveway. Six-year-old Matt confidently pumps the pedals, secure in the knowledge that Dad is right behind him, all the way.

As the two-wheel bike gains momentum, Justin has to jog in order to keep pace while keeping his hand on the seat.

"Don't let go, Daddy," Matt implores, and Justin assures him that everything is fine. A few quick steps later, however, Justin *does* let go, unknown to his little rider, but he continues to run alongside, shouting words of encouragement. Only after they stop does Justin reveal that Matt had made most of the trip *by himself!*

Many a son can recall a similar moment when Dad taught him how to throw a ball, how to swing a bat, and how to master other skills, large and small. Then, in the teen years, Dad took him driving in preparation for getting his license, patiently guiding him through the gears.

Of course Mom was involved in this boy's life, but Dad worked with him on all those special father-son situations. A son learns much from his father's instruction and by watching him in action.

On those occasions, the son usually discovered that he needed to do things *his dad's* way, without talking back or arguing. It's not that the father was controlling—but he was the teacher, and the boy was the student. He was the father; the boy was the son. Each person knew his role and respective place. Living by those rules kept the peace.

Most adult sons also remember learning at a young age that they needed to respect Dad's space and his possessions. If the boy used Dad's tools, golf clubs, or fishing equipment, he was expected to return them in good condition, with no signs of undue wear and tear. And some of Dad's places were definitely off-limits!

Those recollections do not portray a mean and demanding father; nor do they present an idealized portrait of a father who works especially hard at being involved in his son's life. He's just a typical dad, a good father of his generation, doing what fathers do as they rear their young sons.

Fast-forwarding a few decades, most of those sons continued to feel the father's presence whenever they performed one of those skills that he had so painstakingly taught the son years earlier. And when they stepped onto the father's turf, into his domain, they were still careful to do things Dad's way and to respect his space. As an adult, the son acted out of honor, not fear. And even if he disagreed with Dad's way of doing something, the son usually kept quiet—it wasn't worth the hassle.

So at the father's death, we might assume that those feelings would end, that the son would be free from seeing his father at every turn and still seeking his approval. But he isn't, much to the son's surprise.

POSSESSIONS

Usually the uneasy feelings of walking uninvited into Dad's territory or of sensing his disapproving gaze emerge soon after the funeral, when the children and their spouses have to dispose of their father's stuff. If their mother has already passed away, the father had all that was left of their worldly possessions.

"The chair, bed, and mattress were easy," explains Ralph, "but we struggled with the stack of photo albums, each one packed with memories of Mom and Dad together and of our family. Most of the pictures from winter Florida trips during their retirement years featured strangers to us. So those snapshots around the pool, at a friend's birthday party, in a restaurant, and on a golf course held no value now that Dad was gone. Yet it was difficult to put them aside, to discard them. Each time we made such a decision, I felt guilty, as though Dad might catch us in the act. These pictures had meant a lot to him; who was I to treat them so lightly?"

"Fact: It takes a man to teach a man how to be a man. Fact: Most men grow spiritually and in every other way when another man takes an interest in his life and unconditionally accepts him. Fact: While a man might be resistant to a woman's urging out of principle, he is more likely to be open to another man out of example and identification. Fact: Men will ask questions and admit their lack of knowledge and life skills with other men quicker than with women."

—PETE ALWINSON. "AS THE MEN OF THE CHURCH GO, SO GOES THE CHURCH." KEY LIFE (FALL 2002), 10.

For most men, dealing with the father's possessions means trying to discern what to keep. It's difficult to throw away anything that held value to him. In fact, almost every man we interviewed mentioned keeping a few of his father's possessions as mementos. Several had photographs; many kept tools. Phil M. told how his father was a WWII hero, having flown several missions in the Pacific. Recently Phil asked his mother if he could have his father's medals. She told him that he would have to stand in line because his older brothers had made the same request. Phil says, "I did get his silk map from flying over the Pacific. It is framed and hangs in my office. But the memento that is most precious is Dad's wedding band. I wear it as *my* wedding band. My mother gave it to us before Janie and I were married. That meant a lot to both of us."

Len also has his father's wedding band. Mark values the letters his father wrote, and he has a model of the airplane his father flew before WWII. Oliver kept his father's uniforms. He explains, "Dad wore these blue uniforms with his name on them. He was a shop foreman most of his life. So I kept those because that's how I remember him. I also have a fishing reel— we used to fish a lot together."

Dick H. remembers splitting his dad's tools with his older brother. He adds, "I've got his old iron bar that I remember him using to dig tomato posts. We'd put in the garden together. It was hard work."

Mateen bought his father's car from the estate. At first he just thought he would be getting a good vehicle with low mileage, but the car came to mean much more. He says, "The car was a tangible part of my dad's life. Every time I would go into the garage in the morning or come out of church, I'd see the car and immediately think about my dad. So that became a touch point for me in helping me work through some of my feelings."

Mateen also has an unusual memento. He explains, "Most Muslims have lots of prayer beads. They're also called 'worry beads' in the Middle East, from people fingering them as a nervous habit. I kept one set of my father's beads and hung them in the car around the rearview mirror. It has been a helpful reminder, a goad or signal, for me to pray for my mom and my siblings."

Paul V. wears his father's shoes; he keeps getting them resoled. Art does the same. Spike wears his father's watch to important occasions because he knows his dad would have enjoyed being there.

In Remembrance of Me

"In contrast to some, I have only fond remembrances, solid foundations, and great anticipation of whatever heaven promises that is better than heading out together on a brisk morning to catch a trophy northern pike. This has been a happy reminder of sacrament for me as well—'This do in remembrance of me.' Every time I cast one of dad's old plugs, I'm once again reminded of him and what we shared over our years together."

—Dr. Jay Kesler

Whether it's the flag off the casket and a small barber pole from Dad's old barber shop (Ty), his Bible and the sweater Mom knitted for him (Kurt), lodge medallions (Ed), a blue signet ring (Jeff B.), a pearl-handled pocket knife (Roger), police guns, holster, and stars (Dave), a grain scoop, old horse collar, and cow bell (Jeff R.), a clock he made for Tom's wedding present (Tom L.), or two Purple Heart medals (Bill W.), these objects, the father's possessions, keep men and their dads together. In a sense, touching the object is a way to stay in touch with him. One son says he honors his father when using his father's table saw. Another says he feels his father working alongside when he uses his hoe in the garden. Several say they almost sense their father's presence when they wear an article of his clothing. These revered objects remind men of their fathers and help them stay connected.

PLACE

Familiar locations have poignant associations attached. Remember revisiting the elementary school where you had skipped up the stairs, listened to wise "old" teachers, and raced at the bell to recess on the playground? Although you discovered that everything was much smaller and less intimidating than you remembered, the place brought memories, both pleasant and painful. Or you may have returned to the camp where you spent a glorious week every summer, swimming, canoeing, performing silly skits, pulling outrageous pranks, and chasing members of the opposite sex. Even the dining hall still had that distinct aroma.

Certainly there's no place like home for evoking memories. A visit to the apartment or house where a child learned to walk and read and tie shoes brings a flood of feelings. The backyard with "home plate" still bare, the corner of the room where you sat and watched Saturday cartoons, the kitchen where the family would encircle the table at breakfast—each room holds its stories. And certain places are forever tied to our parents: a structure, a room, a workbench, or even a chair.

My parents had left our family house long before my father's death. Downsizing and failing health had moved them to a smaller house, then to an apartment, and then to a retirement village. So when I would visit Mom and Dad, and then just Dad, only some of the furniture recalled my childhood. But they owned a cottage in northern Wisconsin, and there I felt almost overpowered by my father's presence.

After our parents died, ownership of the cottage transferred to us five siblings, and we soon set about the formidable task of cleaning, repairing, and modernizing the place. By sharing the cost, we were able to complete projects that Dad had wanted to do but couldn't afford. So it felt good to replace the roof, level the floor, and repair the doors. Other changes were more difficult. When we removed the lamps from the porch and the curtains in the bedrooms, I felt guilty, as though we were violating Mom and Dad's space. With every improvement and change, I found myself wondering, "What would Dad think?" And just the other day, I referred to "Dad's workbench" in the boathouse. In that place I see and feel him at every turn. (Dave Veerman)

"James Dobson's father died in 1977, the same year Focus began. Before he died, he prayed for his son and counseled him to try radio instead of television because it would take less time away from his family.

"'You never quit trying to please your dad even when he's gone,' Dobson says with a smile. 'I think about him now. I'd like to bring him here. I'd like to show him around. I'd say, "Dad, look at what you influenced!" I would really like that.'"

—PATRICK KAMPERT. "STILL IN FOCUS." *CHRISTIAN READER* (NOVEMBER/DECEMBER 2002), 30

Possessions and places help us recall memories, pure and bright. These memories help us rethink our lives and how we want to live. For many, memories are stronger helpers than talking.

John D. and his father shared a great love for the outdoors, and they often went fishing, spending countless hours together floating down the river. John inherited this interest and some of his father's tackle. John remembers, "The summer after my dad died, I was fishing the river with my son. He was sitting in the back of the boat, much like I had done with Dad. Suddenly we both had the same feeling, and Matt said, 'Something weird's going on.' We felt as if Dad was in the boat with us."

A storage shed, the basement, an office, a church pew, or his place on the couch—we can feel Dad's presence in certain, special places. And sometimes just being there feels like being with him, for better or worse.

DISCIPLINE

In many homes, Dad is "large and in charge" and expected to be the tough disciplinarian, especially with the sons. Innumerable boys have heard their mothers' ominous threat, "Just wait till your father gets home!"

Sons whose fathers were strong disciplinarians often report that fear of Dad's discipline kept them out of trouble. And sons whose fathers were exemplary role models in certain areas find themselves making the same positive choices quite naturally. The father can influence his son's moral and ethical decisions.

As adults, we are still the children of our parents, for good or bad. And most adults still consider what their parents would think about how they have chosen to live and behave. Men, especially those relatively close to their fathers, find their thoughts drifting to what *he* would think. Spike reflects this truth when he says, "I always wanted to please Dad. Suddenly I couldn't please him anymore. But still, every day, I try to live up to the standard he set."

Jerry L. says, "I miss my dad most when I do something wrong. He would either let me know not to be too hard on myself or help me figure out how to fix it."

Dad may be gone physically, but still he influences his son.

"*All throughout my growing-up years I knew that my dad was a dynamic and confident and decisive and successful, capable person. But I also knew that at the center of his life, the core of the core of the core, his was a heart yielded to God. His was a heart that was surrendered to God. He didn't have a legalistic and sort of heartless, religious kind of faith. He had a dynamic and very genuine faith in God.*

"*Some of my richest memories of him when I was a little boy are standing next to him in church. When it would come time to sing a hymn, he'd grab the songbook. I remember looking up out of the corner of my eye and seeing this very strong, autonomous man singing, 'All to Jesus I surrender. All to him I freely give. I surrender all. All to him I owe.' I can remember him singing, 'I have decided to follow Jesus. No turning back. No turning back.' Can you imagine the impact of seeing that and feeling those feelings?*

"*Dad had a deep respect for the Scriptures. He read the Scriptures to our family at every dinner meal. He had passionate feelings about the local church. Our struggling little congregation had a lot of problems, never grew much, and never had many dramatic conversions or answers to prayer. It was just sort of a boring little church that barely survived. But my father did his best to do what he could to breathe life into it . . . and I saw him serve and give . . . I never recall a single time when I sat next to my dad in the twenty-some years that I went to church with him that the offering plate went by with him not contributing to it. He gave a full tithe of his earnings and gave thousands of dollars beyond that. He was considered an easy touch for anyone who had a need. He had a generous heart and was a faithful giver and contributor to things of God. Can you imagine the impact this had on me?*"

—BILL HYBELS. ADAPTED FROM A SERMON AT WILLOW CREEK COMMUNITY CHURCH ON FATHER'S DAY, 1997.

BLESSING

Closely tied to discipline is parental approval, the pronouncement that the child is good. As we grow and mature under the
watchful eye of our parents, we want to make them proud. Trent
and Smalley have written and spoken eloquently about the necessity of "the blessing," the sincere statement by a parent to the
child that the boy or girl is good and special.[1] Indeed, those who
do not receive this blessing may spend a lifetime trying to earn it.

Our interviews revealed that a man adjusted more easily to
the next phase of life, though not necessarily with less pain, if
he believed that his father approved of him, his wife, and his life
direction. This carries tremendous weight. Many felt and were
confident of the father's approval, even if it was never voiced.

In healthy families, fathers and sons bond during approval situations. After the Little League game, Dad pats his young second baseman on the back and says, "Great game. You hustled
and really made some good plays today. That tricky ground ball
you scooped up—that was special. I'm so proud of you." Or at
the end of the pier, Dad demonstrates how to cast the bait.
Then, giving the pole to his son he says, "Now you try . . . that's
it . . . good job!" Or Dad checks out the report card and
exclaims, "Super! All that hard work paid off!"

"I miss my father the most when I see Mom alone, when I see
her trying to do things he did," explains Todd, "and when I see
my nephews because he loved them so much, and when there is
a big game on TV, and I am left alone to watch it. And I miss
him when I succeed in my profession and am looking for a 'well
done, my boy!' *I miss you, Dad!*"

In those families, sons grow up enjoying and expecting words
and hugs and high fives of affirmation and approval. Sure we
need and enjoy them from Mom, but a son thirsts for Dad's
approval, like dry soil needing rain.

A few years ago, a famous professional golfer-turned-TV commentator shared his father-son relationship with his television audience. He told how he was driven to gain his father's approval, and even though he had won several prestigious tournaments, he never seemed to do well enough to please his father. Only when his father lay dying in the hospital did he finally "bless" his son.

Chuck had a similar experience. His father was a perfectionist—when Chuck did something with him, it had to be perfect. This made Chuck very insecure and unable, at times, to accomplish the smallest task without the fear of not doing it right. As a young adult, he often would second-guess something that he had done a hundred times. For example, Chuck might measure the same piece of wood three or four times for fear of cutting it wrong. Or he might measure the spot to drill a hole at least three times. He could remember his father being on his case as a boy, especially if he were to cut the wood wrong or drill the hole off-center. If Chuck were to do it right, still he would be wrong because it wasn't *good enough*. Even today, decades later and several years after his father's death, in the middle of a project, Chuck wonders if his work is "good enough," feeling the negative consequences for messing things up. Although Chuck has made tremendous progress in dealing with these insecurities, every now and then those feelings appear when he least expects them. Make no mistake—this need for Dad's approval is powerful.

> *"I miss my father when I realize that I no longer have the option of picking up the phone to share thoughts with him as I did in the past."*
>
> —DR. KEN BOA

Jim G. tells of building a kitchen table. He was about three-fourths done but had stopped because of his father's funeral. Then, he couldn't get back to the table for several months. When he finally returned to the project, he remembers thinking, "I'm doing this because Dad was a carpenter. This is woodworking, and by working with wood, I am connecting with Dad—I'm being like him." I also realized that although Dad was gone, I still wanted to do this in a way that would make him proud, even though he couldn't see it." Then he adds, "You never really get rid of wanting to please your dad and wanting to make him proud. A couple of years later, I put a deck on the house. Again, I thought about doing it in such a way that would make him proud, just as if he were still alive."

"As I stood at his grave, I thought of how Dad had been a Chairman of the Board of Deacons, a Youth for Christ board member, one of the founders of a Youth for Christ chapter, and Chairman of the Youth for Christ Board. He had been a foreman and a plant manager and had held various management positions. But none of that was on his grave marker. I just saw 'John Hutchcraft, Husband and Father.' I guess that after the smoke clears and life gets sorted out as it does at the end, that's what really matters. None of the other titles usually matter on your gravestone. But, above all else, husband and father was what my dad was."

—RON HUTCHCRAFT

When a father dies, so, too, dies his ability to approve, compliment, affirm, and bless. We know that, of course, but we feel the loss. We know we cannot tell Dad about any new accomplishment and receive his compliment and pronouncement of blessing. But we still find ourselves acting as though he would be proud of us if he knew what we had done, if he could see us now.

LIFE LESSONS

The "over the shoulder" experience shares characteristics with "loss of audience," since both involve the perceived need to interact with Dad. The difference lies in the type of interaction. In "loss of audience," we miss our biggest fan, the one to whom we could always brag about our kids and with whom we could always share our *own* accomplishments. In the "over the shoulder" experience, however, the sense is one of looking for approval and feeling, at times, as though we are treading on forbidden territory. Invading Dad's turf, making changes and messing with his stuff, we almost expect to be caught and disciplined.

Of course we need to grow up, to become adult men in our own right, free to make decisions and live without the fear of being second-guessed by our fathers. But that's much easier said than done, even when the father-son relationship has been warm and positive. And, as we have already discussed, a man's relationship with his earthly father affects how he relates to his heavenly Father. Unfortunately, some hear the word *father* and remember harsh judgment, perfectionism, and even abuse. For them, an eternal, all-powerful, and all-knowing "heavenly Father" is not a pleasant image. Thus, many men avoid God, believing that he only wants to judge and condemn and hurt them. They continue to hear the message, "Wait till your Father gets home!"

So what lessons can we draw for our own efforts at fathering? Here are a few suggestions.

Receive the Blessing

Men who never felt affirmed by their fathers will live with a hole in their hearts. Smalley and Trent write, "Most people who have missed out on their parents' blessing have great emotional difficulty leaving home. It may have been years since they have seen their parents, but unmet needs for personal acceptance can keep a person emotionally chained."[2] These men need to find this blessing elsewhere, since receiving it from their fathers is no longer possible. Other men, father figures, may give the blessing to a child or young man. Often an older brother, a favorite uncle, a foster parent, a coach, or a youth worker will fill this role. For an adult male, however, the process is a bit trickier, since we see other men as our peers. Yet we still may be able to find an older man to serve as a mentor and confidante.

"Most sons I interviewed were willing to forgive almost anything if they could hear—in whatever way and at whatever age—the genuine affirmation of their fathers. These declarations of love and pride salved wounds the son had received in childhood. They tended to reduce tensions in the father-son relationship. And they often served as a hand up as well. Sons who received the blessings of their fathers frequently spoke afterward of feeling more mature, more fully adult. It was as if the father was representing not only himself, but the adult male world, and the son had been accepted into it."

—NEIL CHETHIK. *FATHERLOSS*
(NEW YORK: HYPERION, 2001), 260.

Whatever the case, the ultimate source of this fatherly blessing should be God, our heavenly Father. We need a fresh look at the truth of God's *real* nature and attributes. Regardless of the actions of earthly fathers, our Father in heaven loves us, wants only the very best for us, wants to guide us the right way, and pronounces us "good." His affirming blessing can free us from the burden of having never been blessed by Dad. If we need proof of God's love, we need only look to the cross (see John 3:16).

Read this powerful poetic description of seeing God as "Abba," "Daddy."

CIRCLES OF PAIN

One morning I stood at the window
Made cold from the outside rain
And rubbed a circle on the steamy glass,
Exposing, beneath, the pane.
Through my circle, I saw my father,
Climb routinely into the car.
His job would keep him distant,
His work would take him far.
"Of course, your father loves you.
Can't you see how he provides?
Just accept," my mother told me,
"That he keeps his love inside."
So I too learned the business and
Made love a transactional art.
I sold my grades to buy his time.
I played sports to buy his heart.
Yet, I imagine once my father
Made his own circles on the pane.
I know his dad had left him.
He had not heard from him again.

And I imagine that in his young heart,
He had made a solemn vow:
He would love his sons and give them time.
He would break the cycle now.
Yet in his noble ambition
My dad soon too became
Another father, the circle unbroken,
The patterns still the same.
And as time passed by and our numbers grew,
I left home in my own car
I never returned to mend the fences.
I never returned to start
To share the pain I felt inside
And the grief I had learned to stuff.
No, it was more than I could handle,
But less than I could bluff.
Still something inside me beckoned,
For I too had come of age.
I now had children of my own
That I had begun to encage.
No longer a boy, yet still I desired
A father's voice acceptive of me.
Too often I wanted to scream and shout;
Too often I wanted to flee.
It was time to go, and wisely so,
To find that for which I yearned.
I couldn't make sense amidst the pretense,
Until this I finally learned:
That once, two thousand years ago,
The sky burst forth in rain,
But it was a Son who had gone to work,
And a Father who felt the pain.
It was His whisper that drew me close,

A voice which caused no shame.
I found the Father of my great search,
And ABBA is His name.

—Dr. Ken Canfield,
National Center for Fathering

Give the Blessing

The lesson should be clear as we consider our own families: We must bless our children. That is, we must help them feel good, wanted, and worthwhile. This means making the powerful pronouncement by expressing approval verbally, often, with statements such as, "Good job!" "You're special." "Thank you for doing that. I really appreciate you." "I love you!" There are hundreds of ways to bless our kids.[3] We want them to grow up *whole*, not "hole." As Robert McGee says, "To be a good parent, just be the father you wish you had had."[4]

"I am so thankful now that even when my father was difficult to be with, even when he didn't return calls, I still made the effort. I paid for his hospitalization; I paid for his going to the nursing home; I held his hand for eight-and-a-half hours the day he died and had him cuss at me for praying for him. Emotionally I didn't get my 'cup filled up,' by my dad, but I am so thankful that I did everything that I could to try to solidify the relationship. So now I can look back with no regrets."

—Dr. John Trent

At key moments in their lives, Mitzie and I would consciously bless our children, expressing our love and our approval of their life direction. At those times, we would give the child a present and a prayer. I felt healed in doing this because I don't remember receiving my father's blessing—it was absent in my life. (Bruce Barton)

Reinforce Strengths

The "blessing" pronounces a child as "good," regardless of performance. Closely linked are approval and guidance. This means helping our children discover their strengths, abilities, and gifts and encouraging them to develop them further. Affirmation encourages and motivates. We should look for opportunities to affirm our kids—when they performed well in music or a sport or in school (not perfectly, just well). Then we should express our approval and pride in their performance. But we should also affirm character traits—loyalty, honesty, faithfulness, courage, compassion—glimmers of those should bring praise.

Teach Skills

We don't learn skills by watching. We must be taught. Simply defined, a skill is an action preceded by the words "how to." Skills can range from "how to tie your shoes" to "how to be a good friend." One of our most important parenting responsibilities is to teach our kids the skills they will need later in life: how to solve problems; how to make decisions; how to manage money; how to get along with the opposite sex; how to understand the Bible; how to know what God wants.

As many parents do, Gail and I would pray with our girls at bedtime. We cherished those times, of course, and have many poignant memories of special moments. I remember thinking one night, however, that as important as those times had been, I had never taught my daughters "how to" pray. Sure, they could listen to me and copy my words, but I hadn't taken the time to explain what those phrases meant and why I had said them in that order, or even why I had said them at all. So I broke down prayer into three parts and used this as a way to teach them "how." First, we say "thank you" to God, thanking him for everything he has done for us and for who he is. Next, we say "I'm sorry," asking God to forgive us for when we have disobeyed him or ignored him. Then, finally, we say "please" and ask God to help us. Through this process, my girls learned a vital spiritual life skill. (Dave Veerman)

Teaching skills must be intentional. We need to work at it.

Delegate Authority

Managers live with the principle of delegation. They know that the most effective way to accomplish a large project or to build a company is not to do it all themselves but to recruit a team and assign each team member an important task. Then they allow the team members to do their jobs. Delegation frees a manager to manage, and it frees him or her from the burden of doing it all. But good managers also realize that what they must delegate is *authority*, not ultimate responsibility.

> "I miss my dad the most when I need advice."
>
> —MAX LUCADO

In other words, if I have a job to do and I decide to do it through others, I still bear the ultimate responsibility for the successful completion of that job. I can't simply assign it to someone else and then forget about it. As a responsible manager, I need to check occasionally to see if we're on track. And I need to be ready to step in if we're headed the wrong way. But I need to give the workers the authority and the tools to accomplish their tasks.

The same should be true in our role as father. We should look for ways to download responsibilities to our children (appropriate to their age, of course). At the same time, we should delegate to them the *authority* to carry out these tasks. This will teach skills and will build self-esteem. And it will give us fresh opportunities to bless them.

I remember when Dad allowed me to drive the station wagon, with the whole family in it—Mom, Dad, my younger brothers and sister— all seven of us. I was nervous but thrilled. Dad trusted me! (Dave Veerman)

Delegation will also help our adult children establish a peer relationship with us. That is, we will be able to relate as fellow adults and not just as father-child. This won't keep our sons from "looking over the shoulder" after we're gone, but it will free them from guilt and fear.

Relax

The final lesson to learn from the "over the shoulder" experience is the necessity of being laid-back and relaxed with our kids. This just means letting kids be kids, letting them act their age. Certainly we must exercise discipline when necessary, but we should not demand perfection. We aren't perfect, and (surprise, surprise) neither are our children. So if we expect them to be perfect, we will discourage and frustrate ourselves and them. And we will build insecurity into their lives.

Frank says, "Among my parents' boxes, I discovered a file of old papers and pictures from my childhood. Evidently they were expecting to put the items into a scrapbook someday. As I examined each fragile sheet of paper, I had to laugh at the sentence structure and drawings. I sure wasn't a budding Shakespeare or van Gogh. Yet I remember Mom and Dad praising my work and then hanging it on the refrigerator. They didn't expect me to write or draw masterpieces, and they affirmed me. I felt good about myself."

Another man remembers "helping" his father with various projects. He says, "I'm sure that I wasn't much help, especially before high school. But Dad allowed me to participate, and I grew through the experience." We need to relax and let our kids be themselves and act their age.

Feeling as though Dad is looking over our shoulders can be unnerving and, in some cases, debilitating, especially if we never received his blessing. But we can learn from this experience as we receive our heavenly Father's blessing and then relate to our own children—blessing them, delegating authority, and allowing them to be kids.

WHAT DO YOU THINK?

1. What areas of your father's world were off limits to you?
2. When are you most aware of feeling as though your father is looking over your shoulder? Are these positive feelings or negative ones?
3. Why do you think you feel this way?
4. What one or two events stand out as times that your father gave you his blessing?
5. What other adult males "blessed" you?
6. How do you give the blessing to your children?
7. When was the last time you delegated authority to your child? How did he or she do? How did you respond?
8. When do you tend to be a perfectionist?
9. What can you do to be more relaxed with your kids?

9

SENSING THE LEGACY

Knowing What We Have Received and What We Can Pass On

More than two decades ago, Dan Fogelberg wrote and recorded the hit song "Leader of the Band," a moving tribute to his father. The title was not just figurative—Dan's dad, Lawrence Fogelberg, served as a high-school band director, and he had provided the inspiration and motivation for his son's music career. The song continues to be a favorite because it reflects how many men feel about their dads. In the now-familiar lyrics, Dan admits his life has been "a poor attempt" to imitate his father, but he concludes with the punch line, "I am a living legacy to the leader of the band."

Intentionally or not, sons copy their fathers. Certainly we inherit many of Dad's characteristics—stature, hairline, profile, eyes. But we acquire much more by following his example. In fact, *adopted* sons often hear, "You're just like your father," and it's true, even without the biological link. Remember trying to shave or dress or walk just like Dad? Over the years, long after we've stopped consciously trying to imitate him, the similarities grow. And now we're a lot like Dad, even without trying. Like Fogelberg, we may end up as "poor imitations," but we are like our fathers nonetheless—living legacies.

Sons become aware of their father-likenesses at memorable moments and during life passages, but we sense them most at the funeral and the months to follow as we sort through memories and belongings. For then we reflect on his life and see how he has been reflected in us.

HERITAGE

At this point we often consider our lineage, our family heritage, as well. Remembering Grandpa and perhaps even great-Grandpa,

---

"When the young man with the guitar sang the song about his father in the Assembly Hall at the University of Illinois last fall, more than a few eyes became misty. Lately, more than a few ears have been attracted to the song, which is in Billboard magazine's Top 10.

"And more than a few people have had their lives affected by the 'Leader of the Band'—Lawrence Fogelberg.

"His 30-year-old son, Dan, one of the hottest acts in the contemporary music business, recorded the song last year for his Innocent Age album. The LP has since gone almost double-platinum, and he just wound up a tour supporting its release.

"Larry, a long-time and much-heralded band conductor in Peoria and Pekin, among other places, first heard the song about a year ago at his Peoria residence. 'Dan was home and played a tape of it,' he said. 'I wasn't supposed to hear it. I've been breaking up ever since . . .'

"'Dan says it's amazing how many people say they wish they had the foresight to tell their fathers of their love for them while they still could,' his mother, Margaret, said."

—MICHAEL MILLER. ADAPTED FROM "LAWRENCE FOGELBERG, THE LEADER OF THE BAND." PEORIA JOURNAL STAR (MARCH 7, 1982).

---

we look for significant patterns, sets of characteristics handed down generation to generation.

Many discover, with gratitude, a legacy of faith and faithfulness, passed from father to son and father to son—families centered on Christ and his service. Some, however, see a nearly unbroken chain of character flaws, problems, and struggles. Those sons seek to alter the course, resolving to leave a positive legacy instead.

Because sons tend to copy their fathers, for better or worse, these are important thoughts and resolutions. Each father leaves his son a legacy in values, morals, lifestyle, and relational style.

"When a dad loves God, when a dad lives for God, when a dad manifests faith in God by participating in the work of God, when a dad cheers his sons and daughters to orient their life around God, it is a powerful legacy. In my opinion, that was his most important and significant legacy to me."

—BILL HYBELS. ADAPTED FROM A SERMON AT WILLOW CREEK COMMUNITY CHURCH ON FATHER'S DAY, 1997.

VALUES

Seminars and books for parents challenge them to take the parenting role seriously, especially when it comes to modeling values and teaching skills. Being a parent is a high calling, and God expects mothers and fathers to do it well.

Parents come in all varieties, with some taking their responsibilities more seriously and performing them more proficiently than others. But all parents, whether consciously or unconsciously, strongly influence their sons and daughters, especially in regard to their values.

When children are young, Mom and Dad exercise complete control over their diets, wardrobe, and schedules. Good parents also work hard at teaching right and wrong and what is important in life.

During the adolescent years, these conscientious parents begin to release the controls, allowing and expecting their maturing teens to make certain decisions and then to live with the consequences of their actions. The ideal is a smooth transition to adulthood. But most parents find this passage far from "smooth." In fact, during the teen years, many parents begin to wonder if they have influenced their children at all. Adolescents push and argue and seem to reject everything their parents believe and stand for as they swing away from Mom and Dad's values.

Relax—the move is temporary. Eventually, like trapeze artists, the kids will swing back. Studies consistently show that adult children reflect the values of their parents, what they saw modeled and lived out before them during their formative years.

Remember when you discovered that you had become your parent? Perhaps it hit you when you reacted to pressure the way your father did. Or maybe it happened when you repeated your father's pet phrase or reprimand, the one you vowed never to say. Thus, we know from our own experience that we picked up what we saw in our environment. As Harry Chapin intoned in "Cat's in the Cradle," "My son was just like me. He'd grown up just like me." This tendency for sons to become like their fathers is seen first and foremost in their values.

It is impossible to *not* model values. We reflect our values in the choices we make as we invest our time, our money, and our emotions. What did your father value more: his garden tools or his golf clubs? How do you know? Which place meant more to him: his tool shed or his office? How could you tell? Given the choice, what would he rather do: go on a business trip or stay home with the family? What would make your father the most upset: learning that you failed a test or discovering a dent in the car?

Determining what a person highly regards can be easy. Examining a man's checkbook and schedule will reveal much about his priorities and what he deems important. And seeing how he reacts to unexpected setbacks and losses will speak volumes.

My dad was "the quiet man." He never made an issue out of his devotion to God or drew attention to himself. But every morning he would read his Bible. He would write the date on the chapter break when he finished. When he finished the Bible, he'd start over. I would come down to the kitchen at 6:30 A.M. (rarely), and he would always

---

"The most striking thing about my dad's last days was that he was not all about himself during that time. In fact, he realized what his mission was. At the funeral I saw a tall, distinguished, 30-something African-American gentleman walk into the service. That was Randy, and Randy had been my dad's roommate in the hospital. Over a period of time, my dad had shared Christ with him. As a man who always felt amazed with the sin of his life and that he had been a recipient of God's amazing grace, my dad could never go to communion or take communion without tears in his eyes. He could never sing a hymn like 'The Old Rugged Cross,' or anything about the cross without it choking him up. He was so amazed at God's love for him and God's grace. He shared that with Randy. So my dad's last great ministry was to pray with Randy, and Randy with him, and Randy gave his heart to Jesus Christ. My dad spent his last conscious days on earth helping somebody else be in heaven."

—RON HUTCHCRAFT

"My grandfather opened his desk drawer and pulled out a worn envelope. His eyes twinkled and his whole face smiled in anticipation as he handed it to me. That deep voice reached my ears and heart as the paper touched my fingers. Seventy years of preaching gave his voice a timbre I won't forget. 'I've been saving this for you,' he said.

"At that moment, the 'this' didn't really matter. What mattered was that my grandfather had been thinking about me again. It wasn't the words he said as much as the way he said them that always captured my attention. I have old cassettes of his sermons from which I have made transcripts, but the typed words bear little resemblance to the vitality that flowed through his short sentences, delivered in deep, rolling, measured tones. With Grandpa Wilson, sentences rarely ended with punctuation. They led right into laughter or tears.

"Years later, when I was a young pastor, he would call me sometimes on Saturday nights. All he had to say was 'Hello,' followed by that chuckle, and I knew who was on the other end of the phone line. He usually had one question: 'So, what has the Lord given you for them tomorrow?' I confess that my sermon preparation was often equally motivated by the desire to have a word from God to tell my congregation on Sunday and by the desire to have something to tell my grandfather on Saturday night.

"I was keenly aware, as I held that envelope, that I was receiving blessings. My almost-ninety-year-old grandfather was bequeathing to me objects that represented the treasures he had already given to me through genetics and family patterns: a sense of speechless awe before the Creator that passed through my father and into me; an all-too-real propensity for tears when subjects seem too dear for words; and a deep appreciation for the power of God's Word. The contents of that envelope had to do with that connection of shared faith between us."

—NEIL WILSON

be there—*coffee, cereal, and his Bible. To this day, I try to read the Bible each day. I take that from his example. He also modeled stewardship. Every Sunday he put his 10 percent (and more for missions) in a church envelope. It was the first check he wrote on payday. Today I'm chairman of our church stewardship committee. Giving is one of my highest priorities.* (Bruce Barton)

Now consider what *you* value as an adult and how those values reflect your parents. If faith and family stand at the top of your list of priorities, they probably were highly valued by your mother and father.

We asked each man we interviewed what legacy he received from his father. Here are several of their answers relating to values.

Jim Wilson says, "I want to talk about my heritage. Dad loved his children dearly and let us know that in numberless ways. He was involved in what each of us did, and he managed to get near us during those important passages in our lives. He was a prayer warrior for us. He was an active member of our Bible translation team, along with Mom. Dad took chances, moving out in faith and confidence. He was a trainer—an encourager." Jim's father modeled the importance of family and faith. Thus Jim has spent a lifetime in Christian service as a missionary with Wycliffe Bible Translators. He has also passed those values to his son, Neil, the next generation.

"My father's love for the Lord, his integrity, love of people, generosity, and work ethic stand out as supreme examples of his life to me," reports Jim F. "One character trait standing out even beyond all but the first of those was the magnanimous manner in which he dealt with a serious employee problem, even after having been slandered by the employee to the point that many thought he should have filed a suit against the man. What a lesson!"

One man says that he witnessed unconditional love in action when his father graciously forgave a prodigal daughter and welcomed her back. This man's sister had been estranged from the family for seventeen years while involved with a cult. He says, "Talk about unconditional love. I believe my sister's involvement with the cult triggered my dad's sickness that eventually resulted in his death. It affected him deeply. Yet he forgave her."

In answer to the question of what he received, Jeff B. answers, "Trust in God. Dad wasn't a big Bible toter and quoter, but he certainly trusted in God. He also exemplified boundless love for us, with discipline. (He had definite boundaries.) The image of God came through Dad. And he taught me to live life to the fullest, to enjoy every day."

According to Mark S. this inheritance was life-changing. He explains, "I received a great spiritual legacy from my parents. Their conversions to Christ and resultant commitment

---

"I would have cherished my father's admonition if he had lived another two decades, but there is something about a person's final words that make them particularly significant. The fact that they were some of the last words Dad ever said, 'I'm not struggling to stand, I'm struggling to kneel'—seared them on my soul . . .

"Dad knew he had prayed all his prayers, and it was time to leave the next generation in the hands of God. My father expended his last bit of precious life force and energy to assemble a gift he gave as we knelt knee to knee.

"Some fathers deal with their sons eyeball-to-eyeball; others, nose-to-nose. In the end, my father dealt with me knee-to-knee."

—JOHN ASHCROFT. LESSONS FROM A FATHER TO A SON (NASHVILLE, TENN.: THOMAS NELSON PUBLISHERS, 1998), 202–3.

to ministry truly changed the course and destiny of my life and those of my entire family."

Paul L. also recalls his spiritual legacy. He says, "I want to strive to be like this man who lived every moment wanting to serve and praise his Lord."

For a father and son, the influence and similarities can be almost amazing—"Like father, like son" is more than a cliché. So we shouldn't be surprised that we acquire our father's values.

LIFESTYLE

Closely related to values is lifestyle—our habits and hang-ups, the way we live. Good parents seek to both model and teach good morals to their children. Naturally, they try to protect their children from danger, nurturing them physically, emotionally, and spiritually. They also try to teach them the difference between right and wrong and keep their kids out of trouble. Looking back, we can see our fathers' influence here as well. They did their best to steer us in the right direction.

"The legacy I received from my father? A deep faith and an example of hard work."

—MAX LUCADO

Some men enjoy a recreational legacy; that is, they credit their fathers for interesting them in a hobby or sport. Jim F. recalls, "When I was 17, my dad wanted me to learn to play golf. And when he said to do something, you did it right then. Through golf, I got to know my dad—we became much closer. Dad had to play for his health, but it changed our relationship." Jim developed his game and became an outstanding golfer, even touring for a while as a professional. Jim adds that

The Touch

When I was just a lad at home
I'd often hear folks say
"You look just like your dad. You know"
And that sure "made my day"
They said I combed my hair like him
And sounded like him too
they said I walked and talked like him
Hey "What can ya do?"
Some said I had my father's eyes
And that I had his grin
I even had a copy of
The dimple in his chin
I was quite pleased to look like him
Indeed he was a rock
It was a compliment to be
A "chip off the Ole block "
So many folks looked up to dad
For all the things he did
I've tried to follow in his steps
Since I was just a kid

-◆-

And so we stayed and watched some more
until it became twilight
His hands still cupped around my ears
As his arms held me tight
And even to this very day
My ears do not get cold
For I still feel my father's hands

And his warm touch of old
I still feel the touch of his hands
that warmed me with his love
and he still feels my little nudge
from heaven up above

FROM A POEM WRITTEN BY JEFF JENKINS AT THE DEATH OF
HIS FATHER, FEBRUARY, 2003

his legacy also included "Dad's strength of character, integrity, and his ability to build lasting relationships."

As mentioned previously, from his father, John D. inherited an interest in fishing. He says, "Dad gave me the river and his love for fishing. The river became my passion. He took me down the river; then I took him down. Fishing has become a great joy shared with the entire family. My kids cherish their memories with Grandpa."

Several men mentioned music as a significant part of their family heritage. They remember Dad standing with the choir, singing in a quartet, or leading the orchestra. Music played an important role in many families—informally, at special occasions, and performing together.

Lifestyle, of course, includes much more than recreational activities. How fathers lived at home, at work, and in the community—their reputations—also provide powerful images. For example, Chuck describes his father's legacy as mostly negative: harshness, perfectionism, and dominance. In contrast, Roger reports receiving, "a good and balanced work ethic." He adds, "I appreciated Dad's tenacity and endurance, his humility, and the way he treated Mom."

Many of the men we interviewed mentioned their father's integrity as their ethical legacy. John D. remembers, "Dad would tell me, 'If you say you're going to do something, do it.' He also showed me that hard work gives joy. And he taught that I should be steadfast—don't quit—work through it."

"My father modeled integrity, hard work, and being frugal," says Bill W. "Dad was extremely strong in these areas."

Jim W. has a similar response. He recalls, "Dad modeled a sense of hard work, a sense of integrity. (Your word is your bond.)" Jim adds, "Dad had chosen to work in public service, an 'other' orientation. He was unimpressed with what money had brought others. I also learned the importance of estate planning—Dad had done the will and had made sure his home was paid off."

"My father's legacy was faithfulness, dependability, consistency, a work ethic, and, above all, integrity," explains Russ. "My father used to say, 'All you have is your word. Don't promise what you can't do. Be all the time who you say you are.' And he used to say, 'When you're out of the house, you represent the family.'" Today, as the head of an effective and well-respected urban ministry, Russ exemplifies these same character traits. He is known for consistency, dependability, and integrity as a man of God.

Spike says, "My father was a fair man, and he was always level with everyone. He treated each person the same. In a phrase, he was a *good man*. I want people to say the same things about me that they said about him." They do.

Some men remember their father's legacy as mixed. These sons consciously work at *not* replicating their fathers in certain areas. Bill J. says, "Dad always loved people. In that way, I'm a lot like my dad. He could remember names—people were important to him. And he had a zest for life. In his heart, he wanted to be a loving guy, even though he messed up his life. Years before he died, I pledged to God to be a different kind of father than he was. For example, I tried to create a family where we dealt with conflict." Bill is a loving man, like his dad, but unlike the example he saw, Bill has become a godly man and a faithful father.

Bill K. has a similar reaction. He says, "Dad was a kind man with a kind heart towards people. And he left a legacy of three good sons. But he was an alcoholic. Because of that, I never drink."

Dave, Bill's brother, echoes that thought when he says, "By his bad example, Dad taught me to stay way from alcohol. I respect that history. He also taught me a lot about loneliness—you

> "My *father left a legacy of spontaneous humor, his love of good friendships, and his vivid imagination.*"
>
> —DR. KEN BOA

don't have to be lonely and hold it all in. I determined to be the opposite of him in many ways."

My father was a perfectionist and very demanding. I suppose he got that from his father. When I would mow the lawn, he would only comment on the part I messed up. Though I had the same reaction as my father to notice the missed sections, I determined to be different. So when my boys would cut the grass and miss a spot, I would discreetly fix it later. I didn't want to give the impression that there's no way to please Dad. I tried to always thank them for doing their chores and say "nice job" a lot. I had to bite my tongue by not criticizing (like my dad) when I first saw a problem. (Bruce Barton)

We can find ourselves acting like our fathers especially when facing challenges similar to the ones he faced. Thus, like Bill J., Bill K., Dave, and Bruce, we may have to make a concerted effort to be different. Those men have successfully rejected their legacy of a self-destructive lifestyle.

RELATIONAL STYLE

Another area where a son mirrors his father is relationships, especially how he treats his wife and children. Many of the interviewed men expressed appreciation for what they saw in how their dads reacted at home.

For example, Jeff R. says he appreciates his father's faith and "his relationship with Mom and his kids." This has helped Jeff be a better husband and father.

Paul V. explains, "From my early days in youth ministry and in my family growing up, the goal of my life has always been to love my wife and be faithful to her, to be as good a father as I can be, and to allow my children the opportunity to put their own faith in Christ. I learned these principles from my parents."

His father's example of keeping his family as a high priority made an impact on Phil V. He says, "From Dad I learned the importance of family. His legacy includes devotion to God and to family."

Al expands on this. He says, "In addition to leaving me the legacy of an immense work ethic and a life of integrity, Dad portrayed that it's very manly to be a Christian father who nurtures."

Mark N. recalls, "Dad loved his wife, his children, and his grandchildren. My greatest encouragement as a husband and father has been the example of my dad. Of course, we know that he was not perfect, but I don't know where anyone could have ever had a better model of a husband and father than I have had. I have prayed for years that I could be half the man to my family that he has been to his."

Even though his father died when Phil M. was in junior high school, he remembers his dad's example at home. He says, "My father worked hard, came home, and rested." And Phil adds, "I'm getting that way. His social life came through his wife. Mine too. I'm not sure this is good or bad, but I'm sure becoming like him."

Relationships, of course, move well beyond the family circle, including neighbors and coworkers. Here many fathers also reflected a solid legacy of honesty and fairness.

- "My dad was honest. He never deceived anyone. And he told me to teach that to my kids."—Mike S.

- "My dad raised me to be a strong Christian man and husband. He showed me what that was by being a living example day after day."—Todd

- "I remember Dad's sensitivity to other people and the reputation he had for doing what was right."—Dick E.

- "Everyone at work knew that Dad was a Christian. (I worked at his plant in the summers.) He wasn't afraid to stand up for what he believed and to live it."—Russ

When discussing similarities to his father, Len says, "My dad was a struggling builder, and he went into business with this guy who ended up being dishonest and running off with twenty-five hundred dollars. This was in about 1948 when twenty-five hundred dollars was a lot of money, so the business was in trouble.

"My dad had pledged to fix a man's house. He went to this man and said, 'I will make good on my promise no matter what it takes.' Dad just sacrificed and went the extra mile to make sure that he delivered and came through and did what he said he would do. Even though he had been wronged and it was really the other guy's fault, my dad made sure that everything was handled rightly.

"I hear stories like that when I go home. My mom and step-dad are still in the same church, and people still talk fondly of my father. So I really appreciate him. I hope I've inherited some of those qualities." He has.

Some fathers model sacrifice and what it means to give one's self to others. As Ralph recalls, "Dad showed me selfless service to people inside and outside of the church. And he exemplified strength in suffering, leadership, and a zeal for independence." Ralph continues, "I also learned, 'Don't feel sorry for yourself; solve the problem!' Dad had a joy in giving too. He was content with so little." Ralph spends most of his time helping others become good stewards of their resources.

Tom E. says, "Dad had enthusiasm for life; he enjoyed people; he was a giver, not a taker; he was a servant; he lived with integrity; he had a simple life." That's Tom in a nutshell.

Jerry W. also learned generosity from his father. He says, "Even though I was only eight when my father died, I think he

---

Marv Veerman.

Strong.

Faithful.

Devoted.

Loving.

Did you know him?

Did you see him hit the homerun? Direct the choir? Wave me around to home as he coached third?

Did you hear him lead a board meeting? Sing a solo? Teach a class? Lead family devotions? Pray? Cheer me on in football?

Did you read his poems? Birthday notes? Letters?

A man of principle, of duty, of faith, Marv Veerman, and he was my hero.

—DAVE VEERMAN

left me his compassion and his willingness to open up and give to anybody anything."

Men described other positive, legacy traits they saw modeled by their fathers. Dick H. says, "I received his spirit of gentleness. He wasn't up or down emotionally. You'd never approach him, and hear him say, 'Get out of my hair' or something. For a farmer and a construction worker, he was a fairly good dresser. He would shave every morning. He was clean; he was gentle; he was kind."

Mateen says, "The passion to keep learning is what I learned from both my parents. To do your best and leave the world a better place than you found it. Two of the tributes to Dad that I heard at his memorial service made an impact on me. First, he lived with integrity and cared about people, and his actions reflected his beliefs. Second, he shunned the limelight and put ego aside in order to do his best." Mateen lives this legacy.

So does Jim G. He answers, "I think the legacy I received is treating others with kindness, being nice to people you don't know when you first meet. That's what my dad did."

The evidence speaks, from our personal experience and from the testimony of countless sons: boys become like their fathers. This reality hits hardest, whether painfully or joyfully, at Dad's death.

So What?

This is a fair question to ask. Besides the obvious answer, that we should celebrate the good we inherited and work hard at minimizing or eliminating the bad, what else should we do? What other differences should "legacy" make in how we live?

Quite simply, we should consider the legacy, the family heritage, that *we* are passing on to our children—especially in values, morals, lifestyle, and relational style. To help in this process, we can project into the future and think of what our sons and daughters will be like if they copy us. What kind of spouses and parents will they be? How will they relate to their neighbors and coworkers? What roles will they assume in the church and in the community?

We can also take an honest look at the model that we have presented and are presenting. Do our actions match our words? If we *say* God is central to our lives, that spiritual value should be seen in the focus of our time and attention. If we *say* that family ranks high on our list of priorities, then others, especially our children, should know that's true by watching how we treat family members and family times.

"I made a commitment to myself that I would keep my dad's memory alive for my children. I wanted to make sure that they knew him. I accomplished this through photos, unique sayings of my dad's, stories of his war experiences, and regular visits to his grave."

—DON DONAHUE

Hopefully, years from now, our children's answers to the question about the legacy they received from us will echo many of the phrases voiced by Jim, Byron, Jeff, Mark, Paul, and others in this chapter:

- the importance of family and faith
- unconditional love
- trust in God
- strength of character

- tenacity and endurance
- hard work
- integrity
- dependability
- fairness
- competency
- faithfulness
- devotion to God and to family
- sensitivity
- courage
- selfless service
- kindness
- generosity

Even if our relationship with our father was bad, we should look for qualities in him that we can uphold as good. Our children need to see us uphold even that partial or meager legacy. This may enable them to follow in our footsteps someday. It is also a significant way to honor our fathers.

It's never too late to build a legacy.

WHAT DO YOU THINK?

1. Before reading this chapter, what did the word *legacy* mean to you?
2. What does it mean now?
3. When are you most aware that you are like your father?
4. What values of your father do you hold?

5. In what ways do you hope to become more like him?

6. What traits will you work hard *not* to emulate?

7. If your children were asked today to describe your legacy to them, what would they say? That is, what character qualities, habits, and so forth have they learned or are they learning from you?

8. What changes should you make in order to leave a more positive legacy to your children?

10

FACING THE FUTURE
Preparing the Next Generation

As Dan talks about his father's death, he gets emotional for more than one reason. Sure, he misses his father dearly, but he also remembers those final days with joy.

Dan explains, "For ten years, my father and I had talked and debated about Christ, off and on. He was a self-proclaimed agnostic but would give very little rational support for his position. So for ten years I was witnessing to him and countering his arguments with facts and reason. But he was determined and wouldn't give in.

"I visited him one evening in the nursing home where he had been placed temporarily while recovering from a stroke. He was extremely sick and was talking about some of the preparations for his death, like making sure that financial matters were in order and taking care of my mother. So we talked through those issues.

"Then I said I had two more things that were very important to talk about. He asked what they were, and I answered, 'We need the power of attorney to conduct your affairs for you.' He asked what we had to do, and I told him that I would draw up the paper for him to sign. Then I said, 'The other question I need to ask is if you know where you will be after you die.'

"Dad answered, 'Yup, I am going to be in heaven.'

"He had been fighting me for almost ten years on that so I said, 'How do you know that?'

"He answered, 'Because you told me.'

"I said, 'You believe that?'

"'Yup.'

"'Do you really believe that?'

"'Yup.'

"Then I said, 'Well, then, let's seal it and make it perfect.'

"Dad's hands were just totally skin and bones, and they were shaking. His hands looked like those of a survivor of a Nazi concentration camp of the '30s. He folded his hands, and together we prayed the sinner's prayer. I just couldn't believe that the Lord was letting me experience this.

"I had to ask, 'Why do you believe now?'

"And Dad answered, 'Because of you telling me that this is true!'

"All those years of arguing and talking apologetics. He was a hard case. In our church, the pastor usually invites people to come to the front and pray right after the service. For a couple of years, I went up every week asking for prayers for my Dad's salvation. And my wife and I prayed daily. So God was really working, and I felt so privileged and blessed to be able to see that. I was just astounded when Dad actually submitted to Christ. I figured that he was just lost and I would never see him again.

"I walked out of that place just floating. It was amazing—amazing grace. After all those years, Dad finally surrendered to the Lord!"

Ten chapters ago, we began at the side of a bed where a father lay dying. And in this, our last chapter, we stand at another bedside.

The death of Dan's father signaled the end of a long story, a lifetime of being a boy, a man, a husband, and a dad. Yet it was the beginning of another, infinitely longer and more glorious life—with his Savior.

Death is tragic and painful—when loved ones die, we mourn . . . and we should. But those who know Christ can also celebrate, confident in the reality of heaven, eternal life, and a future reunion. Dan knew that his father was absent from the body and present with the Lord (2 Corinthians 5:8).

"Nothing can really blunt the sharp pain of the loss of a parent. Two things, however, make my father's death an accepted experience of life rather than a dark trauma. First is the 'blessed hope' spoken of by the apostle Peter. I am confident of seeing Dad someday in the rather near future because of this central tenet of the Christian faith.

"Second is the daily sense of satisfaction that we did not have any unfinished agenda when he died. There was no anger, resentment, unkept promises, regret, words to interpret or recount."

—Dr. Jay Kesler

During our interviews, many men expressed joy in their assurance that their dads were in heaven. These sons knew where their fathers stood with God and thus were confident of their eternal life. And because these sons had also trusted Christ as Savior, they knew they would one day be reunited with their dads.

That's God's Good News—death signals not the end but the beginning! Losing a father brings pain, there's no denying it—shocks and aftershocks of grief and a myriad of feelings. But knowing what lies beyond the grave brings hope and courage.

That was the experience of Jeff R. He says the most important part of the funeral was "the confirmation of our hope in Christ—the Truth." He adds, "We knew that Dad's death wasn't the end but the beginning."

Ralph and I had taken turns spending time with Dad during his final days. And, on separate occasions, we had celebrated Communion with him. Dad knew he was dying and actually wanted to hasten the process—he felt so bad.

Because music and faith had been important to him, I would play tapes of gospel quartets and choirs, featuring styles and songs I knew he would appreciate. And from time to time, we would talk about the next phase of his life. I remember asking, "Dad, what do you want to do when you get to heaven?"

Without hesitation he answered, "I'm going to rest." He was so tired—tired of being weak, of trying to breathe, of being a "burden." After a short pause he added, "Then I'm going to sing." (Dave Veerman)

Many sons don't have that assurance, however. In our interviews, they wondered aloud about the father's destiny.

One is Tom T. He says he's not sure where his father stood with God. Then he adds, "That was my earthly father, but I have a heavenly Father. Those are two different beings completely. My real father figure was the Lord. I don't know if I'll meet my earthly father on the other side—that's up to God. But I think that when we get to heaven, it won't matter. We're constricted emotionally and mentally here because we have finite senses. But when we get to the other side, I think it will be a whole different experience. So I try to leave that for then."

One man reflects what many surely feel: "I always tried to rationalize my father's salvation. I thought, 'How could God not accept such a good guy?' But I know the Bible. It pains me to think that I might not see him in heaven. The fact that my father might not be there led me to question a lot of things at the time of his death. But it also made me open the Book to read it and understand it."

Regardless of how long our fathers lived, their respective lifestyles, and their professions of faith, the critical question we must answer concerns what we will do with the time we have left. That is, how will we live until it's *our* turn to die?

RIGHT NOW

When a father dies, reminiscences flow as we look to the past. Yet eventually we need to get on with life, to live in the present and prepare for the future. We can learn from how our fathers lived and died, but we must make the most of our own living years. This is a profound way to use the past to move into the future.

No one is guaranteed a long life, but most of us hope that many years will pass before we face those final moments. In any case, our time is limited, and we should ask what we can do to apply the lessons of our fathers' lives and deaths.

We've touched on this often throughout this book, but now we come to the conclusion of the matter. The journey is ending, and we must choose how we will *now* react to what we have seen and learned. Here's how some men have responded.

- Chuck says, "I had built up so much anger toward my father, and I wanted to drop it on him. I began going to counseling, and that has helped a lot. When I was finally able to give myself grace, I was able to give it to him." One result of his father's death was Chuck's determination to be even closer to his grown sons and his grandchildren.

- Paul L. answers, "My father's death strengthened my relationship with our grown children as they witnessed my dad's love for his family. And it has increased my communication with my siblings since Dad no longer can share the family news."

- Oliver reflects, "Sometimes I ask myself, *Will my kids be able to handle my death?* Usually I answer yes because they saw what I did, and yes because, hopefully, when this happens I will have given them some opportunities and prepared them in that kind of way. And that makes me feel grateful to God."

- Mateen says, "Because I'm more aware of the passing of time and the preciousness of it, I've become more intentional in carving out time with the family."

Others told of specific actions taken. Len and his wife, for example, decided to spend quality time with their sons. Len reports, "We just did this big trip out West with my boys, just the four of us, and went to all the national parks—the Grand Canyon, Carlsbad Caverns, and Zion National Park—all the way out to California. It was like a nineteen-day road trip. We were the Griswold family from *National Lampoon*. We just lived in the car, but the boys had a blast.

"Thinking back, I remember three or four trips with my dad; after his business got established, he was able to do that. One time we went to Washington, D.C., and I remember him standing in Arlington Cemetery, looking out at those rows of crosses and just weeping. That's a vivid memory of my father, of course, he having fought in World War II.

"Another time he took us to New York City, and that was quite an adventure. We were there probably four or five days.

"Then the capper was when my sister graduated from high school. (She is closest to me in age.) We went on one of those American Express trips to Europe, the whole family—three days in Madrid, five days in London, four days in Paris, and a couple of other places.

"I watched my father transition from this world to the next. He took one final breath and entered an unexplored existence just waiting to be experienced. Exactly forty years before . . . my father was lying in another hospital room, fighting for his life. For all intents and purposes, the doctors had given up on him. My mother had been advised that, apart from a miracle, her husband was going to die.

"Years later, my father shared with me how he had pleaded with the Lord to spare his life—not because he was not ready to die, but because he was convinced that he had not yet accomplished the purpose for which he had been created . . . On his deathbed, he pleaded for one more chance at life—one more chance to make his life count for eternity. The Lord saw my father's tears. He heard his prayers. And he healed him . . .

"For twenty-nine years I chose rebellion over repentance. Before he died, however, my father realized the answer to his prayers—I surrendered my life to Christ and to his calling. I'll never forget the day Dad told me how proud he was of what God had done in my life. With a twinkle in his eye, he said, 'And I had a part in that.' And so he did. Not only am I a product of his prayers, but throughout the forty years that God added to my father's life, Dad modeled what it meant to be a fearless defender of the faith."

—HANK HANEGRAAFF. RESURRECTION (NASHVILLE, TENN.: WORD PUBLISHING, 2000), 157–58.

"Those are my most vivid memories—travel and just being in certain places with him and experiencing things for the first time together. So remembering that helped me make the decision. That, and having my wife say, 'Come on, come on. We've got to live life now. Yes, we need to save for the future and be careful and be wise. But come on. Let's live now. We're going to blink, and our boys will be gone.'

"So that has been fun. We have plans to try to squeeze in more trips to build family memories."

Jim G. had another response. When his son was twelve, Jim did a rite-of-passage ceremony with him. He explains, "We talked about Christian manhood. I made it clear that he had my approval and that he was becoming a man in my eyes.

"When I was my son's age, I would work on my dad's construction sites. My dad always talked about the guys who weighed two hundred pounds and were V-shaped. I was a lot more slender than that. Thus, I always felt as though I never was quite manly enough in my dad's eyes because I didn't have huge shoulders or biceps. So I wanted to make it clear to my son that I viewed him as becoming a man. I also said that if he wanted to make me proud, all he had to do was follow God's will for his own life. Nothing else was necessary.

"I'm sure that the desire to clearly state those things to my son came from always wondering if my dad was proud of me because he couldn't figure out what I did in my job in the ministry. It was foreign to him."

Those men translated their experience into action. We can do the same.

Finishing Well

Our children may be well past the age for taking family camping trips (like Len) or for instituting rites of passage (like Jim). But we're not done yet.

Life has often been compared to a race. For some, the finish line comes much sooner than expected. For others, it seems distant. Some shoot out quickly at the starting pistol; others stumble out of the blocks. Many struggle along the racecourse, with painful strains, unexpected obstacles, and other setbacks, while others seem to sail along. Regardless of our pasts or where we now stand in the race, however, we owe it to God and to our children to finish well, to finish strong.

"I want to live my whole life like that. I want to love with much more abandon and stop waiting for others to love me first. I want to hurl myself into a creative work worthy of God. I want to charge the fields at Banockburn, follow Peter as he followed Christ out onto the sea, pray from my heart's true desire."

—JOHN ELDREDGE. *WILD AT HEART* (NASHVILLE: THOMAS NELSON PUBLISHERS, 2001), 199.

Centuries ago the Apostle Paul wrote, "No, dear brothers and sisters, I am still not all I should be, but I am focusing all my energies on this one thing: Forgetting the past and looking forward to what lies ahead, I strain to reach the end of the race and receive the prize for which God, through Christ Jesus, is calling us up to heaven" (Philippians 3:13–14). Keeping our eyes on the goal, the finish line, motivates us to run with endurance, courage, and faith. We *can* finish strong!

Imagine the time has come. The family has gathered in the funeral home for a private viewing. Peering into the final resting place, one by one, through their tears they see your lifeless form. A few moments later, they sit in a rough circle, just in front of the casket and reflect on you and their remembrances. If that somber event were to happen tomorrow, what do you think they would say? Supposing it takes place several years from now, what do you hope they will remember? And, if you have boys, imagine their responses *when their father dies.*

One father answered this way: "Certainly I want my children to remember me as a man of God and as a faithful and loving husband. I hope they know that I loved my Lord and that I loved their mom. But I also want them to say, 'Dad was there!' So I've tried to be with each one at every significant event— recitals, games, plays, concerts, crises, and celebrations."

From today, right now, until we hit the tape, we should run well and run strong.

"Straight as he was by nature, this pure-bred Iowan was also straight because of grace. At the stage in life when many Iowans worry (and with good reason) about where to spend their winters, he got excited about Evangelism Explosion. He died in the western part of the state at the house where, seventy-four years and two months before, he had been born. He was there to help his older sister come home from the hospital, and, characteristically, he would not let her pay for the groceries they picked up on the way. He died as he had lived: a straight man at the end of a straight road who knew the straight highway to God."

—DR. MARK A. NOLL. "AT THE END OF A STRAIGHT ROAD." CHRISTIANITY TODAY (MAY 17, 1993), 19.

AND THEN

We also should consider the ending, the actual finish line, and the possibilities. So here's a tough question: How will you die? And the follow-up is just as tough: What lasting impression of those moments will your children remember?

"It was the final letter he wrote us. The ALS and cold weather had nearly killed him. Denalyn and I had rushed home from Brazil and spent a month eating hospital food and taking shifts at his bedside. He rebounded, however, so we returned to South America. A day or so after arriving, we received this letter.

January 19, 1984

Dear Max and Denalyn,

We were glad you all made it home OK. Now settle down and go to work. We enjoyed your trip to no end. Even your spending the nights with me.

MAX, YOU AND DENALYN ALWAYS STICK TOGETHER, WHATEVER HAPPENS.

Well, there is no need of me scribbling. I think you know how much I love you both. You all just live good Christian lives and FEAR GOD.

I hope to see you all again on earth—if not, I will in heaven.

Lots of love,
Dad

"I've envisioned my father writing those words. Propped up in a hospital bed, pen in hand, pad on lap. Thinking this would be his final message. Do you suppose he chose his words carefully? Of course he did.

"Can you envision trying to do the same? Can you imagine your final message to those you love? Your last words with a child or spouse?

"What would you say? How would you say it?"

—MAX LUCADO. HE CHOSE THE NAILS (NASHVILLE, TENN.: WORD PUBLISHING, 2000), 149–50.

No one knows, of course, the exact answers. Every man hopes to display courage and resolute faith at that moment of truth, but pain and drugs and fear can move us in the opposite direction. Still those are good questions to ask, for they help us prepare, now, for the end, then.

As Jacob lay on *his* deathbed, he called his twelve sons to him so that he could bless them and give each one his vision of that son's future (Genesis 49). Jacob knew his boys, and he had a special, God-given word for each one. Imagine the impact of those final phrases. A father's last acts and words can make a lasting impression.

- Mike S. says that his father didn't want to die lying down. He also knew that his wife, Mike's mom, would usually ask him to drink his "Ensure." So, knowing the end was near, he asked her to help him into the chair next to his bed. Then he asked her for the drink. After drinking, he put down the glass and died. What determination!

- John Ashcroft writes, "I'm told that in the emergency room, as the physicians worked frantically to help my father remain in this world, Dad finally gave in. 'Boys,' he said, 'you better just quit; you're hurting me more than you're helping me.' Because my father knew that he had been faithful to the strength and mission God had given him, he was willing to let go when the time came."[1]

So this would be a good time to consider your last impression. Like Jacob, think of each child. What memento will you leave to each? What blessing will you give? What words will you say to your wife and children?

Our closing encouragement to you is simply to allow the loss of your father to help you bring your life into sharp focus. Resolve now to live lovingly in the present, to consider what it will take to finish well, and to prepare for the lasting impression you will leave with your family when you cross over into eternity.

WHAT DO YOU THINK?

1. What do you remember most about the details surrounding your father's death?

2. If you had your wish, how would you like to die?

3. If you knew you had only a day left to live, what main message would you give to your wife? To each child?

4. What memento would you like to leave behind for each loved one? Why?

5. In what ways has your father's death (or reading this book) altered your lifestyle?

6. What does "finishing well" mean?

7. What will it take for you to finish well?

Conclusion

Final Words from the Men We Interviewed

In our interviews with men, we always asked them, "What advice would you give to other men whose fathers have recently died?" We close the book with a sampling of their answers— practical advice and godly wisdom from some of the men who graciously shared their stories with us.

- "Have your accountability group pray a blessing over you."—Chuck Aycock
- "Openly express your feelings with other family members. Go to a place and literally cry out your feelings to God. The hurt never goes away and can't be filled by other people—only by your heavenly Father."—Jeff Bishop
- "Talk about it with other men whose fathers have recently died; process the experience. If you didn't have the chance to say good-bye to your dad, do it." —Roger Cross
- "Think of what you would want your dad to be proud of you doing."—John DeGroot
- "Use Father's Day as a time to remember your dad and celebrate the positives he passed on to you." —Ken Canfield

- "Pass on your dad's legacy as a way of paying tribute to him."—Don Donahue

- "Focus on whatever good you received from and through your father and be thankful for that. Dwell on those things in God's presence with a thankful heart."—Mateen Elass

- "Go back to the search for meaning in life. What really, really counts? What really counts is the end of the book of Ecclesiastes: to fear God and keep his commandments, for this is the whole duty of man. Everything we do is on that track. Then determine the legacy you received from your dad and think about what you are going to pass on to those who come behind you."—Dick Epps

---

"When I closed my dad's funeral and it was time for that last walk by the casket, I turned from the little podium and faced the casket and said, 'Dad, I'll see you at home.'

"And by the grace of God, I intend to do just that."

—HAROLD IVAN SMITH. ON GRIEVING THE DEATH OF A FATHER (MINNEAPOLIS, MINN.: AUGSBURG FORTRESS, 1994), 133.

- "Go ahead and cry. It brings relief and even joy. Focus on the positives, and try to learn so you can share with your children."—Tom Essenburg

- "Families should talk."—Jim Fenton

- "Look at the life he led and find what was good. If he was a believer, be at peace, knowing that all is right."—Marshall Gage

- "Take the best parts of your dad and incorporate them into the way you father your own kids."—Art Greco

- "You can't dwell on 'I wish I could have done X, Y, or Z while he was alive.' That does no good. You need to cross the line. It's over. It's done. You have no control over that. And don't take seriously the words of the well-intentioned. People say stupid stuff, and most advice is worthless. People always try to come up with a reason. The worst ones are those who spiritualize. Also, you can't dwell on the, 'I wish I would have.' Cross the line; it's over; move past."
—Dick Hagstrom

- "Be a benevolent grandfather—love children as though they were just perfect."—Al Hargrave

- "Celebrate everything that was praiseworthy about your dad. Forgive him his faults. Use the occasion to witness for God. Be strong for the rest of your family; let them make some of the decisions and step up to your new role as the patriarch. Be there to help your mom."—Cap Harper

- "Process your feelings and be able to talk about it with someone. I had a couple of friends with whom I could talk."—Bill Jackson

- "Be in touch with your emotions and what they are saying. They will come out at some point in time. Pull your family together."—Dave Kane

- "Whenever you lose someone (the depth of loss is related to the depth of the connection), you need to process the loss. It may take three years. When the waves come, say 'Thank you, Dad, for the memories . . .' Have a conversation but then transfer to God, your 'Abba Father.'"—Ray Kane

"I really wish my dad had given me the gifts of time or tenderness or touch. But he didn't. He gave me some wonderful gifts, but I did not get it all. I don't think he got it all from his dad. I'm pretty sure my kids are not getting it all. I'm pretty sure you didn't get it all. I'm pretty sure your kids aren't going to get it all. So what are sons and daughters to do? There are some options.

"First, you can celebrate the good gifts that your dad gave you and simultaneously stick your head into the sand about the gifts that you didn't get that even caused you pain. A lot of people do this. They idolize their dads. They sort of make them of epic proportions. They diminish or discount any pain that came from them. They just hold them in high esteem and roll along, and I did that for many years with my dad. It's an option—to celebrate the good and discount anything other than that.

"Another option is you can go the other direction and focus on what you didn't get from your dad, and you can work yourself into a dad-bashing lather. And there's a lot of that going around these days, some of it under the guise of therapy. It can get real evil and dark and ugly.

"Or maybe there's a third alternative we should consider. Maybe we could try to look honestly at the gifts our dads gave us and celebrate them and also look honestly at the gifts we didn't get from our dads. Then maybe we can process that disappointment and talk it out with some wise and loving people. Maybe we could feel the pain of all that deeply and grieve it thoroughly, and maybe with the power of Christ we could eventually forgive our dads and let that stuff go and bless their lives.

"This is the path I would recommend. It's not an easy path. It's much easier to just idolize and discount. It's much easier to go to the other extreme and be a dad-basher. I think the only honorable path is to celebrate the good gifts that came our way, then process, grieve, and eventually forgive the rest. That's the choice that I've made, and I hope it's a choice that you'll make someday."

—BILL HYBELS. ADAPTED FROM A SERMON AT
WILLOW CREEK COMMUNITY CHURCH ON FATHER'S
DAY, 1997.

- "Share the good memories of your time with your father with friends and family members."—Paul Lundblad

- "Get help. Talk through the experience. Know that it will take a long time to heal."—Tom Luthy

- "Experience a healthy grief. Do not be afraid to cry and be sad—it honors your father. Do not bury the feelings of pain—it is very normal for it to hurt for a long time. Do not think that you are weak because you grieve—your grief honors your father."—Phil Maxwell

- "Develop the father-son relationship with *your* son. Don't hesitate to express your feelings."—Mark Noll

- "Remember that most parents love their kids. Maybe your dad just didn't know how to express that love." —Spike O'Dell

- "Claim your legacy, your inheritance of those Christlike characteristics that your father had."—Todd Olson

- "Find someone to talk through anything and everything concerning your father, negative and positive—your wife, your pastor, a friend."—Jeff Ringenberg

- "If your father knew the Lord, you can be sure that he is in heaven. Use this to motivate you. Don't feel sorry for yourself."—Mike Swider

- "Grieve fully, and celebrate all that your father gave to you—and minimize the weaknesses he may have had."—Mark Sweeney

- "Distinguish between your heavenly Father, the Lord, and your earthly father. Remember the good; let the bad wash away."—Tom Taylor

- "While it's still fresh in your mind, tell your dad's story into a tape recorder so that you never forget the details."—Kurt Tillman

- "Be the adult and forgive, forget, and concentrate on his good attributes. Don't be afraid to be like your parents. You *will* be like them, but be the good in them and reconcile the bad. Bring it all to the cross."
—Paul Veerman

- "You'll never forget your father, so don't try. Thank God for the good and move on."—Phil Veerman

- "Don't hesitate to cry. Don't be surprised to find a hole in your heart."—Ralph Veerman

- "Be prepared for the emotions. And if your mother is still living, know that her loneliness and emptiness are huge."—Bill Watson

- "Be ready for change. It will put you into a whole new role in your family."—Jim Wilhoit

- "Take comfort in the heritage he has passed on to you. Learn from the good and the bad."—Dan Woodhead

- "Don't be afraid to grieve and get it out. Let yourself feel those feelings—feelings of loss, just deep sadness that this person whose opinion of you is so important, rightly or wrongly, and who gave you life—this huge person in your life is gone. It's sad, so go ahead and feel that sadness. Get it out. Don't stuff it. Don't try to bury it underneath activity or whatever. Don't try to numb that pain with other things."—Len Woods

Appendix A

*The Bible contains hundreds of references to fathers and sons.
This is a representative selection*

FATHERS' ROLES AND RESPONSIBILITIES

Teaching

DEUTERONOMY 6:6–7

And you must commit yourselves wholeheartedly to these commands I am giving you today. Repeat them again and again to your children. Talk about them when you are at home and when you are away on a journey, when you are lying down and when you are getting up again.

PROVERBS 20:7

The godly walk with integrity; blessed are their children after them.

PROVERBS 22:6

Teach your children to choose the right path, and when they are older, they will remain upon it.

ISAIAH 54:13 (NIV)

All your sons will be taught by the LORD, and great will be your children's peace.

Disciplining

PROVERBS 3:12

For the LORD corrects those he loves, just as a father corrects a child in whom he delights.

PROVERBS 13:24

If you refuse to discipline your children, it proves you don't love them; if you love your children, you will be prompt to discipline them.

PROVERBS 19:18

Discipline your children while there is hope. If you don't, you will ruin their lives.

PROVERBS 23:13

Don't fail to correct your children. They won't die if you spank them.

PROVERBS 29:15

To discipline and reprimand a child produces wisdom, but a mother is disgraced by an undisciplined child.

PROVERBS 29:17

Discipline your children, and they will give you happiness and peace of mind.

EPHESIANS 6:4

And now a word to you fathers. Don't make your children angry by the way you treat them. Rather, bring them up with the discipline and instruction approved by the Lord.

Hebrews 12:9

Since we respect our earthly fathers who disciplined us, should we not all the more cheerfully submit to the discipline of our heavenly Father and live forever?

Loving

Genesis 44:30

"And now, my lord, I cannot go back to my father without the boy. Our father's life is bound up in the boy's life."

Genesis 50:1

Joseph threw himself on his father and wept over him and kissed him.

Malachi 4:6 (NIV)

"He will turn the hearts of the fathers to their children, and the hearts of the children to their fathers; or else I will come and strike the land with a curse."

Setting a good example

Deuteronomy 4:40

"If you obey all the laws and commands that I will give you today, all will be well with you and your children. Then you will enjoy a long life in the land the Lord your God is giving you for all time."

Psalm 103:17

But the love of the LORD remains forever with those who fear him.

His salvation extends to the children's children.

Proverbs 19:14

Parents can provide their sons with an inheritance of houses and wealth, but only the LORD can give an understanding wife.

Being a good son

EXODUS 20:12

"Honor your father and mother. Then you will live a long, full life in the land the LORD your God will give you."

PROVERBS 1:8

Listen, my child, to what your father teaches you. Don't neglect your mother's teaching.

PROVERBS 6:20

My son, obey your father's commands, and don't neglect your mother's teaching.

PROVERBS 13:1 (NIV)

A wise son heeds his father's instruction,
but a mocker does not listen to rebuke.

PROVERBS 19:26

Children who mistreat their father or chase away their mother are a public disgrace and an embarrassment.

PROVERBS 23:22

Listen to your father, who gave you life, and don't despise your mother's experience when she is old.

EPHESIANS 6:1

Children, obey your parents because you belong to the Lord, for this is the right thing to do.

EPHESIANS 6:3

And this is the promise: If you honor your father and mother, "you will live a long life, full of blessing."

COLOSSIANS 3:20

You children must always obey your parents, for this is what pleases the Lord.

1 TIMOTHY 5:1

Never speak harshly to an older man, but appeal to him respectfully as though he were your own father. Talk to the younger men as you would to your own brothers.

The rewards of parenting

PROVERBS 10:1

A wise child brings joy to a father; a foolish child brings grief to a mother.

PROVERBS 17:6

Grandchildren are the crowning glory of the aged; parents are the pride of their children.

PROVERBS 23:24

The father of godly children has cause for joy. What a pleasure it is to have wise children.

God as Father

DEUTERONOMY 1:31

"And you saw how the LORD your God cared for you again and again here in the wilderness, just as a father cares for his child. Now he has brought you to this place."

DEUTERONOMY 32:6–7

Is this the way you repay the LORD,
you foolish and senseless people?
Isn't he your Father who created you?
Has he not made you and established you?

Remember the days of long ago;
think about the generations past.
Ask your father and he will inform you.
Inquire of your elders, and they will tell you.

PSALM 27:10

Even if my father and mother abandon me,
the LORD will hold me close.

PSALM 68:5

Father to the fatherless, defender of widows—
this is God, whose dwelling is holy.

PSALM 103:13

The LORD is like a father to his children,
tender and compassionate to those who fear him.

ISAIAH 9:6

For a child is born to us, a son is given to us. And the government will rest on his shoulders. These will be his royal titles: Wonderful Counselor, Mighty God, Everlasting Father, Prince of Peace.

ISAIAH 64:8

And yet, LORD, you are our Father. We are the clay, and you are the potter. We are all formed by your hand.

MATTHEW 5:45

"In that way, you will be acting as true children of your Father in heaven. For he gives his sunlight to both the evil and the good, and he sends rain on the just and on the unjust, too."

MATTHEW 6:26

"Look at the birds. They don't need to plant or harvest or put food in barns because your heavenly Father feeds them. And you are far more valuable to him than they are."

MATTHEW 7:11

"If you sinful people know how to give good gifts to your children, how much more will your heavenly Father give good gifts to those who ask him."

MATTHEW 23:9

"And don't address anyone here on earth as 'Father,' for only God in heaven is your spiritual Father."

LUKE 6:36

"You must be compassionate, just as your Father is compassionate."

LUKE 11:2

He said, "This is how you should pray:
Father, may your name be honored.
May your Kingdom come soon."

LUKE 12:30

These things dominate the thoughts of most people, but your Father already knows your needs.

JOHN 8:41–42

"No, you are obeying your real father when you act that way."
They replied, "We were not born out of wedlock! Our true Father is God himself."
Jesus told them, "If God were your Father, you would love me, because I have come to you from God. I am not here on my own, but he sent me."

JOHN 14:20–21

"When I am raised to life again, you will know that I am in my Father, and you are in me, and I am in you. Those who obey my commandments are the ones who love me. And because they love me, my Father will love them, and I will love them. And I will reveal myself to each one of them."

JOHN 16:23

"At that time you won't need to ask me for anything. The truth is, you can go directly to the Father and ask him, and he will grant your request because you use my name."

ROMANS 1:7

Dear friends in Rome. God loves you dearly, and he has called you to be his very own people.

May grace and peace be yours from God our Father and the Lord Jesus Christ.

ROMANS 8:15

So you should not be like cowering, fearful slaves. You should behave instead like God's very own children, adopted into his family—calling him "Father, dear Father."

1 CORINTHIANS 1:3

May God our Father and the Lord Jesus Christ give you his grace and peace.

1 CORINTHIANS 8:6

But we know that there is only one God, the Father, who created everything, and we exist for him. And there is only one Lord, Jesus Christ, through whom God made everything and through whom we have been given life.

2 CORINTHIANS 6:18

"And I will be your Father,
and you will be my sons and daughters,
says the Lord Almighty."

GALATIANS 4:6

And because you Gentiles have become his children, God has sent the Spirit of his Son into your hearts, and now you can call God your dear Father.

EPHESIANS 3:14 (NIV)

For this reason I kneel before the Father.

EPHESIANS 4:6

And there is only one God and Father, who is over us all and in us all and living through us all.

HEBREWS 2:11

So now Jesus and the ones he makes holy have the same Father. That is why Jesus is not ashamed to call them his brothers and sisters.

HEBREWS 12:9

Since we respect our earthly fathers who disciplined us, should we not all the more cheerfully submit to the discipline of our heavenly Father and live forever?

1 PETER 1:2

God the Father chose you long ago, and the Spirit has made you holy. As a result, you have obeyed Jesus Christ and are cleansed by his blood.

May you have more and more of God's special favor and wonderful peace.

1 JOHN 3:1

See how very much our heavenly Father loves us, for he allows us to be called his children, and we really are! But the people who belong to this world don't know God, so they don't understand that we are his children.

Appendix B

FATHER FILMS

Most movies these days seem to feature plots and subplots that highlight the father-son relationship. Consider, for example, the "Star Wars" series of films and the startling revelation in the third episode that Darth Vader was Luke's father. Because of that knowledge, we search the subsequent "prequels" for insights into their relationship.

Following is a list of movies, some classics and others recent, in which the father-son relationship is a dominant theme. At times we see a loving father portrayed; other films dramatize a dysfunctional relationship. In many cases, the son must deal with his father's impending or recent death.

By listing these films, we are not endorsing them. In fact, you may find that certain scenes or dialogue in some of them are offensive to you or inappropriate for children. Still, these movies tell powerful stories and offer valuable lessons and inspiring illustrations regarding the father-son relationship.

Braveheart

1995   Rated: R

Although the majority of this film is about Scotsman William Wallace and his quest to snuff out English tyranny in Scotland, two important father-son relationships are highlighted. The first is the relationship between William and his father, whose death deeply affects him. The second is between King Edward I and his ineffectual son, Prince Edward.

Breaking Away

1979   Rated: PG

This film tells the tale of four friends trying to figure out their future after high-school graduation in Bloomington, Indiana. Dave, one of the main characters, has a difficult relationship with his father, who sees him as the bane of his life. Their relationship and communication difficulties form a subplot of the film.

Dad

1998   Rated: PG

This serious drama deals with the importance of family relationships and features three generations of fathers and sons. A son moves in with his aging parents in the hopes of making their final days easier. The care he gives them, and his rekindling of that relationship, helps intensify the one he has with his own son.

Dead Poets Society

1989   Rated: PG

This film focuses on a group of boys in a prep school and their relationship with their English professor, who encourages them to "seize the day." One boy in particular wants to become an actor despite his father's ambitions for him. This character, Neil, tries to reconcile with his father.

Death of a Salesman

1985   Rated: PG

Although depressing and disturbing, this film shows the relationship between two men, their families, and their struggles to live out their dreams. One of the main characters lives for and adores his two sons, and the other male character takes little interest in his son.

Field of Dreams

1989   Rated: PG

This ultimate feel-good movie shows the main character, Ray, building a baseball field in his cornfield in hopes that "Shoeless" Joe Jackson will come pitch on it. Ray eventually realizes that he hasn't built the field to bring back the ghost of this player, but the ghost of his father.

Frequency

2000   Rated: PG-13

This is a great film about the relationship between a father and a son. In 1969, fireman Frank Sullivan died in the line of duty, leaving behind his loving wife and six-year-old son, John. But the past is about to change. A day before the anniversary of his father's death, John Sullivan discovers in the house he inherited his father's old ham radio and begins to play with it. Through the electrical static, he finds himself talking to a man whom he discovers is his father. At first neither can believe it, but soon John is carrying on an all-night conversation with his young father. John uses the mysterious radio and clarity of hindsight to save his dad's life in the past—a noble act that creates a devastating wrinkle in the fabric of time that father and son must iron out together. It also clearly shows how much they value their relationship.

The Great Santini

1979   Rated: PG

Based on the Pat Conroy novel, this film tells the story of a Marine fighter pilot who funnels his frustrated desire to fight into creating a tip-top battalion out of his own emotionally battered family. The pilot's adolescent son suffers the most from the father's inability to express love through anything but discipline. This critically acclaimed movie has become a touchstone for dysfunctional families.

The Homecoming

1973   Rated: PG

Based on a play, this film shows the importance of family relationships. It focuses on the return to a bad childhood and how relationships can change.

Hoosiers

1987   Rated: PG

This feel-good movie tells the incredible true story of a small-town high-school basketball team and their drive to become Indiana State Champs in 1954. The film follows the controversial basketball coach who changes not only the team but also the hearts of the people. A subplot involves the relationship between one of the players and his father and highlights the destructiveness of alcoholism in that relationship. This movie clearly shows the strength of a father-son bond.

How Green Was My Valley

1941   Rated: PG

This classic film based on Richard Llewellyn's nostalgic novel shows the trials and hardships of a mining family in a small community. It features the conflict between a father and his sons when they move out and away from the family.

Kramer vs. Kramer

1979 Rated: PG

This film presents an emotional portrayal of the devastating effects of divorce. In this family, the wife leaves her husband and their young son. The situation proves to be especially difficult since the workaholic father has never really taken care of the boy and, in truth, barely knows him. As the two become accustomed to life without Mom, and Dad's parenting skills improve, father and son develop a close relationship. As Dad devotes more time to his son, he devotes less to his work, leading to his being fired. This event coincides with the return of Mom, who wants her son back.

Legends of the Fall

1994 Rated: R

This epic romance is set against the backdrop of WWI and the wide sky and rugged terrain of Montana. It revolves around three brothers who live with their father in the Montana Rockies and how jealousy and war slowly destroy their family.

Life Is Beautiful

1998 Rated: PG-13

This critically acclaimed film portrays a loving father trying desperately to protect his son. During WWII, a family of Italian Jews is taken to a concentration camp. Refusing to give up hope, the father tries to protect his son, physically and emotionally, by pretending that their imprisonment is just an elaborate game, with the grand prize being a tank.

The Lion King
1994   Rated: G

Wild Africa is the setting for this Disney animated tale of a young lion cub. It highlights the strong relationship between Mufasa, the lion king, and his son, Simba. Mufasa's brother, Scar, wants to be the next king, so he has Mufasa killed, and Simba thinks his father's death is his own fault. Simba spends the remainder of the movie trying to overthrow Scar and coming to terms with his guilt over his father's death.

Memories of Me
1988   Rated: PG

In this film, a high-powered surgeon has been estranged from his father for years. After he suffers a heart attack, the surgeon tries to reconcile with his father. Despite their long estrangement, the two slowly begin to understand each other and try to come to terms with their tumultuous past, their different points of view, and, most of all, their mortality.

October Sky
1999   Rated: PG

This film revolves around an idealistic teen who hatches visions of sending his own rockets into space. But equally important to the story is the young man's strained relationship with his coal miner dad, a tough company man who seems committed to everyone but his son. The father is set on seeing his son follow in his mining footsteps and vocally opposes his son's desire to pursue rocketry as anything more than a hobby.

Ordinary People

1980   Rated: R

This film presents a classic portrait of family life in the face of tragedy. Devastated by the loss of their older son, a well-to-do suburban couple tries to rebuild their lives after their younger son attempts suicide.

A River Runs Through It

1992   Rated: PG

In this film about a Presbyterian minister and his sons, the father teaches his boys the importance of religion, schoolwork, and fly-fishing. This movie focuses more on the relationship between brothers, but shows how their strict relationship with their father affects their decisions.

Road to Perdition

2002   Rated: R

In this story, Michael Sullivan, a mob hit man, goes on the road with his son to avenge the murder of his wife and youngest son. We learn a lot about the relationship between Michael and his son, but there is another father-son relationship in this story as well. The son of Michael's boss is the person who has killed Michael's family. This drama is about fathers, sons, and what makes and breaks their relationships.

The Rookie
2001   Rated: G

This film tells the true story of Jimmy Morris, a Texas schoolteacher and baseball coach, who has always dreamed of playing major league baseball. A bet with his high-school baseball team finds him trying out for the majors. Jimmy doesn't have a healthy relationship with his father so he does everything he can to be a positive role model and mentor for his son, Hunter. Throughout the film we see Jimmy try to heal the relationship with his father, while caring for his relationship with Hunter, who idolizes his daddy.

The Royal Tenenbaums
2001   Rated: R

Royal Tenenbaum was a terrible father who had raised three brilliant but very dysfunctional children. Virtually all memory of the brilliance of the young Tenenbaums was erased by two decades of betrayal, failure, and disaster. Most of this was generally considered to be their father's fault. *The Royal Tenenbaums* is the story of the family's sudden, unexpected reunion one recent winter.

The Santa Clause
1994   Rated: G

In this film, Charlie's divorced father, Scott, is chosen to be the next Santa Claus. Charlie and Scott work on their relationship as they become accustomed to Scott's new role and deal with Charlie's mom and stepdad.

Searching for Bobby Fischer

1993   Rated: PG

In this film we see a devoted father who longs to see his prodigy son become a successful chess player. But family struggles ensue when the mother worries that in cultivating the genius, they may be hurting the child. This story focuses on the importance of trust, unconditional love, and discipline between a father and his son.

Shine

1996   Rated: PG-13

This critically acclaimed and award-winning film paints a wrenching portrait of the life of an Australian piano virtuoso and his struggles with his war-traumatized, demanding father, mental illness, and other issues.

Sleepless in Seattle

1993   Rated: PG

Jonah Baldwin misses his deceased mother and is determined to find a mate for his father, who is desperately lonely. This romantic comedy highlights the desire of an eight-year-old boy to see his father happy again.

Sounder

1972   Rated: G

This powerful and uplifting film relates the story of a family of black sharecroppers in rural Louisiana during the early 1930s. The story focuses on the relationship between the father, Nathan, and his son, David. This film about the black experience moves people of all races.

You've Got Mail

1998   Rated: PG-13

In this romantic comedy, a single man and a single woman meet by corresponding via e-mail. The man, Joe, has a strained relationship with his father who continually talks about his many affairs and divorces.

Notes

Introduction

1. James Dobson, "Family News from Focus on the Family" (June 2002).

Chapter 3

1. Elizabeth Levang, *When Men Grieve* (Minneapolis, Minn.: Fairview Press, 1998), 15.

2. Neil Chethik, *FatherLoss: How Sons of All Ages Come to Terms with the Deaths of Their Dads* (New York: Hyperion, 2001), 6.

3. Elizabeth Levang, *When Men Grieve*, 73.

Chapter 4

1. John Eldredge, *Wild at Heart* (Nashville, Tenn.: Thomas Nelson Publishers, 2001), 62.

Chapter 5

1. Elizabeth Levang, *When Men Grieve*, 46.

2. Ibid., 100.

3. Neil Chethik, "A Primal Bond is Broken for Sons When Dad Dies." *Daily Herald* (Naperville, Ill.: Universal Press Syndicate, 1994).

Chapter 8

1. Gary Smalley and John Trent, *The Blessing* (Nashville, Tenn.: Thomas Nelson Publishers, 1986). The authors identify the five elements that form a "blessing": touching in a meaningful way; speaking a message of love and affirmation; attaching high value; picturing a special future; being actively committed to see the blessing come to pass.

2. Ibid., 19.

3. Ibid., 210–17. Smalley and Trent record statements from one hundred homes "that gave the blessing to children." Also, Wayne Rice and Dave Veerman have included a section on "The Vocabulary of Love" in *Understanding Your Teenager* (Nashville, Tenn.: Word Publishing, 1999), 162–63.

4. Robert McGee, *Father Hunger* (Ann Arbor, Mich.: Servant Publications, 1993), 267.

Chapter 10

1. John Ashcroft, *Lessons from a Father to a Son* (Nashville, Tenn.: Thomas Nelson Publishers, 1998), 211.

Acknowledgments

Special thanks to these men for opening their lives to us and sharing their very personal stories and feelings.

Harry Albright
Byron Amundsen
Edwin Asimakoupoulos
Chuck Aycock
Jeff Bishop
John Blumberg
Ken Boa
Mike Bussey
Ken Canfield
Chuck Colson
Roger Cross
John DeGroot
Don Donahue
Mateen Elass
Dick Epps
Tom Essenburg
Jim Fenton
Marshall Gage
Jim Galvin
Art Greco
Os Guinness

Dick Hagstrom
Hank Hanegraaff
Al Hargrave
Cap Harper
Jerry Hatcher
Ray Hayes
Lee Hough
Ron Hutchcraft
Bill Hybels
Bill Jackson
Jeff Jenkins
Bill Kane
Dave Kane
Ray Kane
Jay Kesler
Russ Knight
Jerry Lichter
Max Lucado
Paul Lundblad
Tom Luthy
Phil Maxwell

Rob Mitchell

Mark Noll

Spike O'Dell

Todd Olson

Ed Poole

Ty Propp

Jeff Ringenberg

Mark Sweeney

Mike Swider

Tom Taylor

Paul Thigpen

Kurt Tillman

John Trent

Oliver Trimiew

Paul Veerman

Phil Veerman

Ralph Veerman

Bob Warburton

Bill Watson

Jerry Webb

Jim Wilhoit

Jim Wilson

Neil Wilson

Dan Woodhead

Len Woods

About the Authors

Dave Veerman

A graduate of Wheaton College (B.A.) and Trinity Evangelical Divinity School (M.Div.), Dave has authored nearly 50 books, including *Dads that Make a Difference, How to Apply the Bible, Parenting Passages, Tough Parents for Tough Times,* and *Understanding Your Teenager.* In addition, he was one of the senior editors of the *Life Application Study Bible* and the senior editor of the *Student's Life Application Bible.* Dave is a co-owner of The Livingstone Corporation, a company that partners with Christian publishers to create, write, edit, design, and typeset new products. Dave and his wife, Gail, live in Naperville, Illinois. They have two grown daughters, Kara and Dana.

Bruce Barton

Bruce served in Youth for Christ/USA for 26 years and was Vice President of Ministry Services. For 13 of those years, he also taught youth ministry at Trinity Evangelical Divinity School. Bruce is a graduate of Wheaton College (B.A.) and Trinity Evangelical Divinity School (M.Div. and D.Min.). He was a senior editor of the *Life Application Study Bible* and the senior editor of the *Life Application Commentary Series.* Bruce is a co-owner of The Livingstone Corporation. Bruce and his wife, Mitzie, live in Wheaton, Illinois. They have four grown children—Kari, Jacob, Scot, and Erik.

The Livingstone Corporation

For more than fifteen years, Livingstone (www.Livingstonecorp.com) has been providing Christian publishers with a complete array of services. Their portfolio includes specialty Bibles, devotionals, curriculum, children's products, trade books, reference material, gift books, software, and multimedia packages for any audience.